Pieced from Ellen's Quilt

Ellen Spaulding Reed's Letters and Story

Lengthen out the happy day.

Fondly,

Linda Otto Lipsett

Ellen Spaulding Reed's Letters and Story

Pieced from

Halstead & Meadows Publishing

Ellen's Quilt

Linda Otto Lipsett

Published in the United States of America by Halstead & Meadows Publishing.

Quilt photography by Sharon Risedorph, San Francisco.

Printed in the United States of America.

Title page: village of Ludlow, Vermont, with the Spaulding brick house and attached gristmill in the center of the photograph, 1888.

First Edition.

Library of Congress Cataloging-in-Publication Data

Lipsett, Linda Otto
    Pieced from Ellen's quilt.

    Bibliography: p.
    Includes index.
    1. Reed, Ellen Spaulding--Family. 2. Reed, Ellen Spaulding-
    -Correspondence. 3. Reed Family. 4. Spaulding Family. 5. Women-
    -United States--Biography. 6. Pioneers--Wisconsin--History--19th
    century. 7. Ludlow (Vt.)--Biography. 8. Ludlow (Vt.)--Genealogy.
    9. Friendship quilts--United States--History--19th century.
    I. Title.
CT275.R3533L57   1991   929'.2'0973--dc20   91-16329
ISBN 0-9629399-0-0

Halstead & Meadows Publishing
Dayton, Ohio

My love and deepest gratitude to Barbara Barton Chiolino, who rescued, saved, and shared the pieces of Ellen's story.

Spaulding brick house with its attached gristmill where Ellen grew up in Ludlow, Vermont. Today a post office stands in its place on Main near Andover Street. The man standing on the porch is believed to be Stedman Spaulding.

Ellen Spaulding Reed

"Mrs Cady came and spent one after noon and I have been and helped her quilt two afternoons   she had a great quilting there was a lot of the neighbors there and some of them spoke to me and some went home without as much as saying why do you so (as Uncle Alden said)"

Ellen Spaulding Reed

Leonora A. Spaulding Bagley

"You may give that white bonnet of mine to Leonora
for the baby if she wants it, if you do not want it and
my old dress that she wanted to make a comfortable of
if you have not and she wants it, you know I was going
to do all this business and a lot more but I came in such
a hurry that I could not do nor think of any thing."

Ellen Spaulding Reed

Mr Steadman Spaulding

Ludlow

Vermont

Tell George we wish he would appear to us as he did
once before, but if not to fat the rooster for
thanksgiving and invite us to supper.

I should think ~~Grandsivell~~
could live some where else and let you come
out here

[left margin cross-writing:] We want our love to every body, write often, I went a visiting the other day, dont you want to know what we had for supper, it was boiled potatoes and thickned dig ~~wheat~~ ~~bread~~, my butter and it was good enough for the king

Janesville, July 18th.

Dear Father & Mother,

As it is a long
time since I have wrote you I
thought I would try and write
this morning, and thought perhaps
you would like to hear from
your children in the woods,
The folks are all well, my health
is good excepting a bad cough but
that is nothing. I should like
to know how your ankle is and
what ails it and what you think
about it, It is very healthy about
here this summer, we have had
fine weather, the crops looks first
rate, it was the hotest day yesteday
I ever saw I should think, but we

Acknowledgments

After twelve years of research and travels piecing together Ellen's story, my memories are rich with the faces of the many special people who helped me and the exciting discoveries and adventures on which they led me. I will never forget standing in front of Ellen's grave for the first time ten years ago with Barbara Chiolino; discovering the site of the Cady brick house with Bernard Larson; tramping through ankle-deep mud and treacherous growth to Willard Reed's land in Plymouth, Wisconsin, with Tilmar Roalkvam; touring Chelmsford, Massachusetts, for Joseph Reed's homes with George Adams Parkhurst; or spending a rainy afternoon with Dale Turnipseed on the same farmland Willard originally cleared in Glendale, Wisconsin.

Willard Reed's great grandson Harland L. McWilliams showed me the end of Willard's story, taking me to the little cemetery in western Missouri where Willard finally rested beside his second wife, Lucy. Another of Willard's great grandchildren, Ruth Shanklin, added the visual part of the story, sharing Willard's daughter Katie's scrapbook with nineteenth-century newspaper clippings and photographs of Willard, Lucy, Stedman, Willie, Katie....

I would like to say "Thank you" personally to the following people for the special contribution each of them made to this book: Jane B. Drury; Julia P. Fogg, Chelmsford Historical Society, Chelmsford, Massachusetts; Harold Hanson; James Hanson, State Historical Society of Wisconsin, Madison; Minnie Hanson; Maria E. Harrington; Eunice Hoepker; Bernard Larson; Juliette Lukas, Milton House Museum, Milton, Wisconsin; Mr. and Mrs. Harland L. McWilliams; Warren McWilliams; Polly Mitchell, Shelburne Museum, Shelburne, Vermont; Betty May Momeyer; Walter Otto;

George Adams Parkhurst; Susan Parrish; Harvey and Ruth Shanklin; Jane and Sam Swindler; Mr. and Mrs. Dale Turnipseed. And my special gratitude to my friend Tilmar Roalkvam for the invaluable information concerning the Glendale and Plymouth, Wisconsin area, that he has sent me, as well as the numerous hours that he has spent with me as guide and historian.

Again, my thanks to Charlotte Rau Ekback for her input and knowledge concerning the construction and details of Ellen's quilt.

My appreciation to Ronnie Alperin for her conscientious, caring, sensitive reading and copy editing.

Thanks and love to my mother, Eileen Kelley; to my sister-in-law Sandy Otto; and to my son, Robert A. Lipsett for accompanying me on my trips and for supporting and helping me in so many ways.

And then there is Barbara Barton Chiolino.... What can I say but to dedicate this book to her? She made it all possible.

Linda Otto Lipsett

Contents

Every effort has been made to reproduce the letters as close to the originals as possible. The script chosen most closely resembles that of Ellen Spaulding Reed's own handwriting.

Introduction

This book has its beginnings nearly one hundred and fifty years ago when Leonora Spaulding Bagley completed Ellen's quilt. With its sixty-five inscriptions, this bridal friendship quilt was created to be a keepsake. During the course of time it has become an important document, a book in itself, of Ellen Spaulding Reed's world before her marriage.

Twelve years ago the care of Ellen's quilt became my responsibility. Piecing together the story of this friendship quilt became my personal goal, perhaps even an obsession. I was determined to find letters, photographs, and memorabilia of the quiltmaker and her family. The quilt appeared to have been taken out of the frame recently. The penciled quilting-pattern markings were still visible in the antique-white sashing, the printed 1850's cottons brilliant and vivid. The condition of it made me consider the possibility that the quilt top had been quilted recently — but only for a moment, for when I turned the quilt over, I discovered the cross-stitched inventory markings, L.A.S 6 and L.A.S. 7. Not only were those initials proof of the quilt's authenticity, but they were my only clue to who might be the central person on the quilt even though there was no corresponding "L.A.S." inked on the top.

From census records and genealogy books, I found information about most of the sixty-three people whose names appear on the quilt. But still I could not solve the mystery of who the central person was and how the other names were related. All were from New England, except one — "J W Reed Burke, Wiss." I called the person who had sold the quilt to me. Could she give me any information to help solve the puzzle? "Call Kiracofe and Kile," she suggested, adding that she had bought the quilt from them. Several weeks later, they mailed a ledger to me that had originally accompanied the quilt. It was of a man's daily business records and personal accounts from 1868 to 1872. The owner, Stedman Spaulding, had written his name near the end of the ledger among his expenses.

While copying the ledger, I was searching for a name to fit "L.A.S." Finally I found Stedman's entry of February 21, 1871, "J. Pradox For six chairs for Leonora." Could that be the name (Leonora Spaulding) fitting the initials on the quilt back? I checked the Spaulding family vital records. Then I realized that I had overlooked the fact that the girl who stitched her initials on the back had been preparing linens for her own marriage. Those initials represented her maiden name, but when her quilt block was inscribed, she was already married. "L.A.S." on the backing was "Mrs L A Bagley" on the quilt top.

Months earlier I had mailed alphabetical lists of the inscriptions on the quilt to researchers in the towns inked on the blocks. From Ludlow, Vermont, I received a letter that the last Bagley, Warren Bagley, had died recently. Possibly, I thought, there might be some clue included in his will.

I was in luck. Warren had willed everything to a Mrs. Helen J. Barton, and her name was in the phone book. Sadly, at ninety-four years of age, Mrs. Barton was no longer able to talk with me. In her place, I was given her daughter's telephone number. And that is where this book really begins, for Barbara Barton Chiolino had originally sold the friendship quilt. She told me she had a box of letters that Warren Bagley had kept. She would begin reading them; perhaps they told something of the story of the quilt. Our correspondence began. Each of our communications by mail and telephone increased my excitement and anxiety. The letters were from Leonora Spaulding Bagley's sister and brother-in-law, Ellen E. and J.W. Reed, out in the Wisconsin wilderness. On the quilt, only J.W. Reed was in Wisconsin; in the letters Ellen and Willard were both there.

B eyond my wildest expectations, Barbara sent all of the letters to me. She had arranged them in chronological order. The first letter was dated "September 11, 1854." Before beginning to read it, I wanted to know the significance of that date. The vital records I had hand-copied months earlier now held new meaning:

Ella-Elizabeth, b. Aug. 14, 1835;
m. Joseph-Willard Read, Sept. 5, 1854.

Ellen had written this first letter only six days after her wedding and the very first morning after she arrived in Burke, Wisconsin. I continued reading the vitals:

She died July 12, 1858, at Glendale, Wis.

If that record was correct (and I desperately hoped it was not), Ellen was to die in less than four years, before her twenty-third birthday. I began reading Ellen's letters knowing I held the truth in my hands.

The letters were from the nineteenth century; yet as I immersed myself in them, Ellen, Willard, their family and friends became living people who were struggling day-to-day with real problems. Ellen was lonely, homesick, hungry. As I copied each word that she wrote, I grew more deeply involved in her plight. I wanted to help her, cheer her, send her some sugar, but, like her parents, I could not touch her. I could do no more than continue reading. The distance was too great — her parents' in miles, mine in years.

M y journeys tracing Ellen's and Willard's paths began, from the Milton House to Burke and Glendale, Wisconsin; from Chelmsford, Massachusetts to Ludlow, Vermont. I entered the same door of the Milton House that Ellen and Willard had entered in 1854; I stood where their houses had stood; I walked the roads they walked. And with sadness, I stood in front of Ellen's grave.

Katie Reed McWilliams's house in Archie, Missouri.

The story did not end with Ellen's death. Willard's letters continued. So did my research and my journeys to different places — to Plymouth, Wisconsin; Lathrop, Missouri; and Kansas City, Kansas. But I had a problem: Willard seemingly disappeared after 1885. I could not find where he lived nor a date of death. There were several years of unsuccessful searching. I had one clue to follow: Willard's daughter Katie had died in Kansas City, Kansas. I found her obituary. Three sons were named. I hoped that at least one of them might have had a son carrying on the family name. Again I searched for obituaries, this time of Katie's children. Finally with the third obituary, I discovered a grandson of Katie, a great grand-son of J. Willard Reed. The name "Harland McWilliams" was listed as a surviving son in the obituary; Harland McWilliams's name was also listed in the Kansas City, Missouri, telephone directory.

It was Harland McWilliams who helped put the final pieces of the story together. From his basement he retrieved several old, very worn pages, entitled "Family Record":

> Joseph Willard Reed Born Mar. 25, 1833
> Married Feb. 22, 1859
> Gone Before May 13, 1911.

On the same page was the information for which I had been searching:

Joseph Reed died at Austin May 13, 1911.

At dusk that evening in June of 1985, I stood in front of Willard's simple gravestone at the secluded Austin (Missouri) Cemetery. Next to him was his *second* wife, Lucy J. Reed.

Willard's great grandchildren remembered their great grandmother Lucy Reed as very elderly and living with their grandmother Kate in Archie, Missouri. She had been married to Willard over fifty years when he died. As far as the great grandchildren knew, Lucy was his *only* wife. From their memories of being at Grandma Kate's, Lucy was a presence in the background, a silent one.

If only I could have talked to her.... She touched Ellen.

Linda Otto Lipsett

McWilliams family photo, c. 1926. Back row, left to right: Great grandmother Lucy Cline Reed, Aunt Edith, Aunt Mina, Grandpa Albert McWilliams, Grandma Katie McWilliams, Hazel McWilliams, and Ruth. Front row, left to right: Cline, Warren, Lucien, DeWitt, Mitzie. Photograph found in Katie Reed McWilliams's scrapbook. Courtesy of Ruth McWilliams Shanklin.

Part I

Ellen Spaulding Reed

In the summer of 1854, in the Spaulding household in Ludlow, Vermont, a very special friendship quilt was in the quilting frame. It was to be Ellen's quilt — Leonora's wedding and going- away present for her younger sister. Each of the fifty-five blocks of the *Album Patch* pattern already had been lovingly pieced. Ten of them had been cut on the diagonal for placement along the outside edges of the quilt. The resulting blocks were each inscribed with the appropriate name and town in beautiful old-style calligraphy by one person's hand.

The people represented on the quilt had been chosen carefully; each one held a special place in Ellen's life. Sadly, several of them were no longer living. A quilt of Ellen's loved ones had to include Grandma Rhoda White Spaulding, who had died six years earlier; as well as her future husband's mother, Ellen's Aunt Leonora Spaulding Reed. Aunt Leonora had died in 1835, yet she would not be forgotten on Ellen and Willard's bridal friendship quilt.

Spaulding brick house with double chimneys and attached gristmill in the center of the photograph.

Not only were the inked inscriptions in the center of the blocks significant, but many of the pieces of cloth framing them were very special — pieces from Ellen's dresses, her father's shirts, her grandmother's aprons. After much thought and care, those blocks had been assembled into the top. Wanting the quilt backing to be meaningful as well, Leonora stitched together a pair of pillowcases[1] and one of the cotton sheets she had hand-hemmed and cross-stitched L.A.S. 7 before her own wedding in 1849.[1]

As the penciled meandering vine-and-oak leaves were quilted into the sashing of the quilt, the time for Ellen's departure to the West was growing nearer. When the quilt was taken out of the frame, the separation of the two sisters was closer than they could know.

Ellen bubbled over with excitement and pride, almost to the point of seeming obnoxious. But then to her family, her behavior was understandable. Every girl should have such a time in her life; she was "fixing" for her wedding. She was happier than she had been in her life — next spring she'd be Mrs. Joseph Willard Reed and be going to housekeeping in her own house. And not in Vermont either, but in the romantic new West — Wisconsin, the "land flowing with milk and honey," in the best of society.

Ellen enjoyed being the center of attention. She was the first to go west since her father's cousin George Spaulding had ventured out to Wisconsin Territory in 1840. In fact, it was George who had convinced Willard to leave New England and to buy acres of fine farmland only three miles from Token Creek, in Burke, Wisconsin. At twenty-one, Willard had no land in New England, nor hopes of ever owning any. As a farmer there was no future for him in Massachusetts. He wanted cheap new government land — the best land the West had to offer for farming. Southern Wisconsin looked promising. Although fifteen hundred miles away from home, at the edge of the western frontier, Willard would have family nearby to help him. George Spaulding, his wife, Mary, of the prominent Lawrence family, as well as George's brother Postmaster Nathan Spaulding and his family would all be there near Burke.

Over the years George had been extremely successful. He had gone out to Wisconsin Territory when his only security and safety had been Fort Winnebago, thirty-five miles south; nine years later and one year after Wisconsin's statehood, in 1849, he built a large, two-story building with a tavern downstairs; a store, hotel, and ballroom upstairs. Since George was situated on the well-traveled highway between Madison (the new state capitol) and Fort Winnebago, he had quickly developed a booming hotel and tavern business there at the crossroads of Token Creek. Because of his establishment, Token Creek was becoming an important, flourishing, little village with a mill and an additional two-story, 14 by 18 foot building housing a general store and shoemakers.

For years, George had written Ellen's father, as well as Willard's father, to get together all the money they could and to invest in farmland there in Wisconsin — the best farmland in the country, certain to double and triple in value. He had even mentioned certain properties for sale and their advantages. There was no more government land available, he had explained. Speculators had grabbed up thousands of acres when it had originally come onto the market, but that land was now coming up for sale. Most of it had never been plowed. Then George had written of ninety acres for sale three miles from his tavern. It was a good piece of land with prairie, some woods, and water. The land lay lower at the southern side on the Portage and Hanson roads, gradually becoming higher and leveling off. Most of it was flat or gently rolling, and all of it could be plowed and planted. Across the Portage road the land was much higher forming a hill on which sat a brick house. Down behind the hill were numerous acres of good marsh.

Pencil drawing of Madison in 1852 by Adolph Hoeffler, showing the capitol in the distance at the end of the road, as well as the University of Wisconsin at the far right. Photograph courtesy of State Historical Society of Wisconsin.

The area was beginning to build up. One side of the forty was on the Madison and Portage road, only seven miles from the village of Madison, and three miles south down the road from George's tavern. There was a schoolhouse on the corner of the Portage road, immediately south of the property. The forty south which was on the same side of the road had a nice two-story log house and several barns on it. Across the road from the log house was another two-story log house belonging to F. M. Talcott. Directly across the Portage road from the land for sale and on the hill was Abner Cady's rectangular, red-brick house that also served as an inn. In George's opinion, the ninety acres were a great investment with great farmland. Soon Willard had arranged with George to buy that property and was making plans for his journey west.

Right now Ellen's intended was there clearing, grubbing, plowing, and building a house — a house for her. Ellen was proud of her future husband. Not only was he very handsome at five feet eleven with light-brown hair and clear blue eyes, but he also carried a maturity, integrity, and determination about him well beyond his twenty-one years. He had always been very serious ever since he was a child. His life had been intense, full of grief. His own mother, Ellen's aunt Leonora Spaulding Reed, had died when he was only two. And then seven months later, Uncle Joseph had married Maria Eaton, a good, kind woman, a loving mother for his two motherless boys, but tragedy had settled into their home with Willard's step brothers and sisters, six in all, dying so young.

Letters from Chelmsford, Massachusetts, had conveyed the sad news over the years. In contrast, Ellen's immediate family in Ludlow, Vermont, had been blessed with health and happiness. Ellen still had three of her grandparents living nearby, and it was especially happy within the walls of the huge brick house with Leonora and Thomas and little Austin and James now living there after Thomas's trouble in Reading. It was so much better for Leonora in her condition anyway, with her confinement and lying-in soon approaching.

Time had passed so quickly for Ellen since the spring when her first cousin Willard had come to visit on his way west. Actually, he supposedly had come to see about his share of the money in the Ludlow bank from Grandsire Asa Spaulding now that Willard was twenty-one. But surprisingly and wondrously for Ellen, he had an additional reason. Willard was a practical man. He was going west and would need a good wife. His first cousin was pretty, spirited, and witty, a perfect compliment to his all-too-serious nature. The question was whether Uncle Stedman would consent to the marriage. Would he allow his younger daughter, the apple of his eye, to move to the far west?

Surprisingly, Stedman and Arterista Spaulding had been enthusiastic for their daughter's future. There were great opportunities in the Western Country; they knew that. George Spaulding often wrote from Wisconsin of the rising value of his land, the height of his corn — facts a farmer could appreciate. Like so many other New Englanders, Stedman himself dreamed of going west, but somehow his family had always been too firmly planted in New

Asa and Rhoda White Spaulding's house in Cavendish, Vermont.

England to leave. His ancestor William White,[2] one of the signers of the Mayflower Compact, had stepped ashore in Plymouth, and generation after generation had stayed in New England.[3] There was something more than just the poor farmland, their comfortable homes, their families holding them there — something intangible as if their feet were planted as deeply as their corn, the cycle continuous from harvest, to plowing, to planting the seed but always there, always to live and die in New England. For two hundred years, seven generations now, their families had been there, and few had strayed. Now at fifty years of age, Stedman had the impetus he needed to leave and go west. Even Leonora's husband was talking about buying land in Wisconsin.

Yes, Stedman would give his blessings to Ellen and Willard. In fact, Stedman grew so excited that he began making plans to look into selling his own farmland outside of town. And as soon as Leonora was gaining again from her confinement, he would journey out to Burke, Wisconsin, to see the land for himself. Soon, Ellen had every reason to believe, her mother and father, as well as her grandparents, would be living near her. Best of all, her sister, Leonora, might be right next door.

There was so much to do to prepare for getting married, but that August of 1854, Ellen believed she had plenty of time. Willard had departed by the cars in the spring with goals set of their land cleared and planted and a good house finished before he returned. Most likely it would be one whole year before Ellen would see her beloved again. Then the focus in the household had changed drastically from Ellen's wedding to Leonora's condition. She had difficulties during her confinements. This third child was no different.[4] Leonora's life was fragile. She must stay flat on her back and not be moved for days after she was delivered with only gruel and water for nourishment, every care taken that she recover from her ordeal.

So Ellen must have been very busy and tired caring for a brand-new baby and Leonora, her plans for her fashionable wedding and exciting journey west in the back of her mind.

While Ellen enjoyed this gregarious time with her family and friends, Willard was swinging his axe from dawn until dusk to near exhaustion on his silent, virgin land in Burke, Wisconsin. He felled the trees and cleared a place, hewed the logs, and painstakingly built a one-room log structure for his betrothed. It was a lonely labor. Willard longed for a wife to share this with, as well as someone to help him. Finally his small, crude log house was completed, and a sympathetic neighbor promised to take care of things until Willard returned with his new bride. So an anxious young man hurried back to Vermont the end of August, months ahead of schedule.

Without even a letter or "telegraph," Willard arrived at the Spaulding doorstep in Ludlow about the first of September. Ellen and he must be married and leave for Wisconsin in haste. As reasonable as that seemed to Willard, his plans appeared overwhelmingly impossible to Ellen and to Ellen's mother. Ellen was not packed. She could not have the wedding she had planned. But the best argument — her father had left only a few days earlier headed for Willard's land to see Burke for himself. "To Madison Dane County and to Burk to see Willard J. Reed[5] and George Spaulding and Nathan Spaulding," he had penned into his pocket-size "Book." The next morning at dawn he left for the cars to "Rutland, Sarratoga, Schenectady, Utica, Syracuse...." Ironically, Stedman and Willard may unknowingly have passed each other, Stedman on his way west, Willard headed east to marry Stedman's daughter. Without question, Ellen could not be married until her father returned. But Willard was adamant. They must be married within a day or two. He could not wait — his neighbors in Burke were caring for his livestock and fields, and cold weather might set in soon.

Willard also did not want to take many boxes and trunks back with them. They should travel as light as possible, he informed his intended; Ellen should only take the things she needed right away. The rest could be mailed later. Everything else they needed they would buy in nearby Madison. Since Ellen was going to be living in the best of society anyway, she thought she would need her good things only, so she packed her elegant best dresses, including her silk, a "light lawn," and her "berage delain." [6] Her mother was to send them along with her "linnen" [6] and card box when she wrote for them. Ellen would take with her only the "things" she needed immediately: a trunk of necessities and her "banbox" with her green bonnet and another bonnet with trimmings.

Ellen was terribly disappointed at having to give up her lavish wedding plans. And to think her own father would not be there to give her away! Nevertheless, love won out masking all else, and Ella-Elizabeth Spaulding was married to Joseph Willard Reed (probably within the walls of the brick house in Ludlow, Vermont) on September 5, 1854. [7] Afterwards, Ellen was presented her wedding and going-away present, the bridal friendship quilt from her sister. The next day, Wednesday, September 6, there were tearful hugs and heartbreaking good-byes. Then Ellen and Willard boarded the Central Vermont Train bound for Rutland, Vermont, on the first leg of their journey west. Ellen's friendship quilt with the names of all those she loved was carefully folded in her trunk near her.

Pages from Stedman Spaulding's pocket-size "Book" in which he recorded his journey to Burke, Wisconsin, in 1854.

The couple had had little courtship — only the few days in the spring and several busy days the week of their wedding. They were first cousins; yet the Reeds lived in Chelmsford, Massachusetts, over one hundred miles from Ludlow. Their visits had been years apart. Frequent letters had bridged the distance. Now this long journey west provided uninterrupted time for Ellen to become better acquainted with her husband. They would have four days and nights of each other's company, most of the time sitting side-by-side on the wooden, straight-backed, cushioned seats, the train jostling them down the tracks.

The cars clattered onward. Approximately ten and one-half hours after leaving Albany, Ellen and Willard "got to Buffalo the next morning where [they] stopped to breakfast." [8] Only one day had passed since Ellen had left home, but it had been a long, exhausting twenty-four hours. Sleeping in an upright position on that noisy, lurching train must have been difficult and uncomfortable; yet Ellen, an excited new bride anxious to see her new home, did not seem to complain. With every hour, she knew she was growing closer to her final destination.

After breakfast, Ellen and Willard got back on the New York Central and traveled around the southern edge of Lake Erie past Cleveland, Ohio, to Toledo (another ten-or-twelve-hour leg of their journey). There they "had to ferry across the river," [8] and then they went on all night via the Michigan Southern — the second night without a bed for Ellen. They did not arrive in Chicago until the next noon, where they stopped for awhile. "It rained quite hard." [8] There was no pavement, just oozing mud and deep puddles. The hem of Ellen's dark journeying dress became soiled and soaked, her bonnet wet. But the rain and mud should not have been Ellen's gravest concerns in Chicago. Since the beginning of summer, within the city one hundred and fifty persons a day had quickly and violently succumbed to cholera. Many more were carrying the disease west by train and stage. [9]

Seemingly oblivious to the epidemic, Ellen and Willard were soon leaving on another train and shortly thereafter arriving in Beloit, Wisconsin. This third night of their journey, Ellen finally got to stop overnight, the first time since her wedding night that she had been in a bed with Willard. "The next morning [they] went on in a stage about twenty miles to Milton and there [they] had to stop till half past eight." [10]

Catching up the heavy, gathered skirt of her journeying dress, Ellen was helped out of the stage. Then Willard and she walked up the steps and into the door of the hexagon-shaped, grout Milton House. [10] The inn was innovative and luxurious for the Western Country, but probably not very impressive to Ellen with the stark white-washed walls and crude tables set in heavy ironstone.

In the evening they went by rig one mile west to the depot

at Milton Junction. There they boarded the 8:30 train to the village of Madison, Wisconsin, thirty-five miles north. After journeying almost fifteen hundred miles by train, stage, steamboat, and rig, Ellen was finally nearing her new home.

During those last days, the cars had passed sad-looking houses, many of which were only rude log structures. Some houses in Wisconsin had no windows or doors; there were only ragged, ugly patchwork quilts or blankets hanging to keep out animals and strangers. Others were made of mud and partially dug into the ground. At best, the houses were log structures, two-story ones. Only in the villages and towns were there familiar-looking houses of brick, concrete, stone, or clapboard, and most of them were poorer and plainer-looking than those in the New England towns and villages she had left.

The people out west looked different too. They were from other countries, spoke in other tongues, dressed in crude, peasant garb — in coarse homespun or blue drilling with no bonnets on their heads, only bright, garish kerchiefs. Norwegians, Swedes, Germans — hundreds of them were pouring into Wisconsin, nearly as

Milton House, Milton, Wisconsin; now a museum.

many Norwegians as Vermonters. Still, Ellen could assure herself that things would be different in Burke, with Madison, the capitol of Wisconsin, only seven miles away. She dismissed all the negative things she had seen and thought about her own new world — the real world of happiness, laughter, wealth, fashionable dresses, an elegant house, their own land across the horizon.... After all, they were coming out here to get rich in the West — that was the talk.

At long last the "monster train, like some huge unheard of thing of life with a breath of smoke and flame, emerging from the green openings — scenes of pastoral beauty and quietude" [11] puffed and whistled into the Madison depot. Travel-worn but excited, Ellen and Willard took the stage about twelve miles to Sun Prairie where they stayed overnight. In the morning the couple went by team the five miles or so to their own piece of land in Burke. For the next few days they stayed with Abner and Dolly Cady and their many children. The Cadys lived on the hill across the Portage road on the adjoining section of land (Section 16) in a pleasant, large, two-story brick, which Abner had built from the bricks of his own kiln down the hill behind the house.

It was in this house the very morning after Ellen arrived in Burke, that she seated herself at a table with her ink and pen. On her blue, gilt-edged bridal paper, she wrote a letter to her mother and father, Arterista and Stedman Spaulding, fifteen hundred miles east in Ludlow, Vermont. Then she folded the pages several times until they fit inside her small envelope and addressed it, "Stedman Spaulding, Ludlow, Vt." Ellen held her new blue sealing wax to the candle and pressed a neat blob of melted wax over the flap.

She had no way of knowing that her own father had returned to Ludlow from his journey to Wisconsin on that very same day.

Burke, Sep 11th 1854

Dear Father and Mother

I have taken my pen this morning to write you what kind of a journey we had. We had a very pleasent time and got along well, we got to Albany the first night a little before dark and stoped there to tea, it rained quite hard when we got there. We got to Buffalo the next morning where we stopped to breakfast and that night found us in Toledo where we had to ferry across the river and then we went on and got to Chicago the next noon and when we got there it rained quite hard, we stopped there a little while and then went on to Beloit where we all stoped over night and the next morning we went on in a stage about twenty miles to Milton and there we had to stop till half past eight and then we started on in the cars again for Madison   we got to Mr Fullers[12] about twelve oclock Saturday night   we staid there till Sunday morning and then Willard got a team to bring us out here to Mr Cadys. We are going to stay here a few days untill we get things straitned at home and then we are going to living, the folks here look and act odd to me but they are good and very accomodading to us. Mr Fullers folks were well, they are first rate good folks. I think it is as good looking place here as I have seen any where on the road and it will laugh well at the old Vermont hills and rocks in a few years when there is some good houses built for that is all that is lacking

31

here. I think it is a smart operation that Father could not stay till we got here but then he can come again when we get to living and you can come with him. Willard has not been to Georges yet but is going soon as it is done raining to see what there is there for us.[13] Tell Abner[14] that if he wants to see the fat Duch [Dutch] girls to come out here. Tell Esther[15] she had better come out here before she gets married and get her some reed curtains. We are going to get us some things soon as we find out what to get and can get around to go to Madison. My things come safe all but the banbox and that got wet and smashed so that my green bonnet is spoiled and the other one wet a little but it did not hurt the triming so that I can get that pressed over or get me a new one, which would you do? I am sorry they got smashed but then we had not ought to think that was very bad luck to what some have for we were not sick and that is better than a new bonnet. There was one lady in the cars with us that had had her money stolen and that was what I should call bad luck, she was alone going to Iowa to her husband. We left the Ludlow company at Janesvill[16] I want you should send my things soon as you can get them ready I wish Abner could come with them but do not send them till we have heard from you and you from us again. Willard has writen to Father Reeds folks this morning.[17] as I do not think of any thing more *to write this time. I shall have to close by bidding you good bye I will write more about things next time. write soon as you get this. give our love to all inquiring friends and keep a good share to yourselves*

We remain yours
J W and E E Reed

Within a few days Willard made room inside the log house he had built, and Ellen and he "went to living." But not as Ellen had planned. She was bitterly disappointed in her new house. Never could she have imagined anything like this. There was little more than a bed and bedstead; some crude, make-shift furniture; and pegs on the rough-hewn walls from which Ellen could hang her fine dresses and silk bonnets. Trunks and miscellaneous belongings took up precious floor space. This was quite different from Ellen's idea of how it would be to keep house.

In contrast, Willard must have been very proud of his first home. He had built this cabin from trees he had felled and split on his own land. The house was small but secure and functional, the stone fireplace on one wall for cooking and warmth.

Ellen had been in Wisconsin nearly one week and missed her sister. Her thoughts focused on the familiar brick house on Main Street in Ludlow. There was always so much hustle and bustle going on. And Grandma Haven was always piecing and quilting another new quilt at her house on Pleasant Street, just the next street over. Then Ellen's aunts and uncles and cousins all lived nearby, not to mention her school friends. There had always been so many people around, besides her going calling. "Lengthen out the happy day, Lengthen out the happy day," her calling card read.

Now there was no one but Willard. Willard had to serve

as her only companion, her only friend, her husband, her everything. She had grown so dependent on his company that she felt completely lost when he left for a day to go threshing for a man. On this Saturday she was alone again and really missed talking to Leonora. If she could not yet talk to her sister in person, she would dip her pen into the ink and write her a good, long letter — she certainly had many things to tell her.

Burke September 16th 1854

Dear Sister Leonora

As I have a few leisure moments this after noon I will employ them in writing to you. My health is about the same as when I left home, and I hope these few lines will find you not only as well but better, and the baby (for I supose that is her name yet [18]) and Esther too. Willard is well, he has gone out to Madison to day to get us some things for keeping house, if we had a house to keep I should not care but we have got a little thing such as they call a house out here but it is very small, one room on the ground and one chamber, you think you are crouded to death almost, but if I had as much room as you have got, I should think I was well off, but never mind we shall have more room in a year or two. You may tell Esther that Willard has gone out to get some curtains to put up around the bed but I guess they will not be reed curtains if they are I will send her a piece, tell her if she is able I wish she would take her boy and come out and stay with us this winter   we will try and make her comfortable as we can and I will help her fix for getting married in the Spring. You had better come out this way, there is a farm for sale just across the road from us [19] and, it would be so much pleasanter for me to have you come where I could see you for now I am here all alone and I miss you very much and the boys too   I wish Austin [20] could come out and stay with me this Winter   he would have business enough to attend to if he was here and he would like the fun too it would take him and the dog to keep the cattle and hogs out of the fields and he might card down the old rooster and get the chickens into the sellar when it rained and that would be pretty often for we have plenty of rain here.   I have washed ironed and churned this weeke   I guess you would laugh to see my great plate of butter but I did not commence setting the milk till Tuesday and churned last night and I got about two lbs. of butter and that is pretty well is it not for two cows <u>and one of them with a bell on her neck</u>

and now I suppose you will ask when I baked, the folks do not have any sellars out this way, or at least we have not any so we live city fashion   cook enough for one meel and let the next one take care of its self.   I think it was a smart operation that Father could not stop here till we got here.   I suppose he has got home long before now. I should like to know how he liked the looks of this country. We are going over to the Creek to morow to see George Spauldings folks. I suppose you are all guessing by this time that I am homesick but I am not for I can eat drink and sleep and folks say they can't when they are homesick but I am lonely when Willard is gone, he has been gone one other day this week a threshing for a man that he owed a days work and I expect he has got to go one day next week to work for a man on the marsh. There was a Norwegean woman came here this morning after Willard went away and I could not understand hardly a word she said but at last I found out that it was a pig that she wanted so I went out with her and helped catch it and then she carried it off in her dress before real Paddy style. As I do not think of any thing more to write I shall have to close by bidding you good bye. We send a lot of love to you and all the rest of the folks

   Your Brother & Sister J W & E E Reed

Ellen signed the letter, and then not wanting to end this warm conversation with her sister, she turned the paper sideways and wrote notes in every remaining space:

I want you should write soon as you get this and write every thing you can think of for I want to hear from you very much.

I do not want you should do as Whelers folks do when John 2 & Sarah [21] write home, go and tell all that I

write for folks will laugh if you do   so keep cool
I supose you will see the letter that I sent home so there
is no use in writing about our journey
I am going to write to Mother to night after Willard gets
home and I am agoing to write to Esther and Abner
before long.

There was no more space on her sheet. Ellen folded the letter and wrote her sister's name and "Ludlow, Vermont," on the envelope. Then there was only silence. Nothingness. No one to talk to — but herself.

It had been a surprise to have a visitor that morning, even if she had been an immigrant. The Norwegian woman had come to Ellen's door in a crude dress from the old country with no bonnet on her head; most likely, just a typical, bright kerchief. Ellen had stood in her open doorway in one of her fine eastern dresses. As lonely as she had felt that morning, she was too proud to accept this woman on an equal social level. That they could not communicate easily only exaggerated the differences. There they had stood — two lonely women from two contrasting pasts now brought together for a few moments by a lost pig.

On that fall day, it was not unusual that a pig was running loose on Willard's property. There were few rail fences laid yet. Willard had not yet fenced much of his acreage, as was probably true of his neighbors. His own livestock also wandered off — one of their cows had an iron bell on its neck for the purpose of finding it when it roamed down into the marsh or into the oaks.

It was most unusual for Ellen, however, to have this one-to-one encounter with a Norwegian woman, and that was an experience she knew would impress Leonora. If nothing else, that proved that Wisconsin was a different world entirely from Ludlow, Vermont.

In truth, this woman was Ellen's neighbor. In fact, many of Ellen's new neighbors were Norwegian. And here in Burke, they were now on the same level, even though their cultures and education may have varied greatly. Their virgin land and pioneer way of living reduced everyone to start from the same lowly beginnings. All men and women faced the same insurmountable difficulties and tasks. The base equalizer was *survival*.

F ive weeks later...

Burke Oct. 20 th, 1854

Dear Father & Mother

I write a few lines this evening to let you know that yours of the 10 th was gladly received, also the one you sent the 3 d. We went to Madison last Thursday and Willard found Mr P.,, [22] and got the check, and spoons you sent by him, and we are going again to morrow to cary the last check and get the money on it. He has killed two of his hogs today, and they have got to go to Madison with us in the morning, perhaps you will laugh to think I am going to town (as we call it) with the hogs, but that is not all, we are going with Willards new oxen, and Mr Tallcotts folks [23] are going with us, he has got him a pair of oxen, and they are smart as lightning, he gave $95 00 for them. I am going to get me some things to morrow, for keeping house, for I have not got any thing yet, and now as I have got a house, I shall want some things. Mr Cadys folks calculate to start next Tuesday, and then we shall move up there, and I do not care how quick, for I have lived crouded up long enough. My box of things has not come yet Mr Pettegrew though they would get here by the 5th of next month. Willards finger is getting well but it will take it some time to get good as it was before. I got a letter from Mary Bagley[24] and one from Maria[25] a few days ago they were all well. Maria wrote that her folks had to stay to Groton over night when they went home as it is geting late I shall have to draw my letter to a close. I shall write again next week, and I want you should write soon as you get this and write about every body and every thing for I want to know how you all do and what you are about. I want to know if the baby has got named yet and if she groows any. I am very sory you did not get your daguerreotypes taken to send, for I had thought a great deel of it but you must get them and grandfathers and grandmothers and send out by the first chance you have. I should like to know if Charles and John are comeing out this fall if they are you can send them by them well I must finish and get ready for bed for we have got to get ready to start by sun rise in the morning so good night.

Yours in haste
Ellen E Reed

Ellen included both of her calling cards with her letter before sealing the envelope.

Well, they could laugh all they wanted that she was going to town in the wagon with the two fat hogs butchered only the day before. But those hogs were going to buy her everything she wanted and needed for her new house. And there were so many things she needed — she had come west without even a fork or a knife. Willard had promised with their $50 and the money from the two hogs there should be plenty left over *after* he bought a stove and a plow and an axe. The rest would be Ellen's to buy what she needed.

But for Ellen it seems there always were disappointments in the West. The next day in Madison they had nearly given one hog away at $4 a hundred and ended up hauling the other one back. Ellen did not get her new bonnet or any of the things she had wanted for keeping house. Their fifty dollars had not gone very far. The stove cost $27 and the plow $12 — because Willard had to have the most expensive one, the imported one out of steel so they "scour bright."[26] Then they had to use the remaining money for "some other things such as is necessary in a family."[27] That day Ellen had experienced her first lesson in the West: "there are so many people comeing to this country that they can ask what they are a mind to and folks must have so they get their great prices which they would not if there was any other way to do, and they are plagued to get things any way."[27]

Pencil drawing by Adolph Hoeffler, showing a wagon on a rutted road of Madison, Wisconsin, in 1852. Photograph courtesy of State Historical Society of Wisconsin.

But it appeared to the new settlers in the area that the high prices were only temporary. The St. Paul road had just opened the past May. Till then all goods had been hauled from Milwaukee by teams. That was slow and expensive, and they were still paying those prices. With the train coming everyday, prices ought to be going down. Besides, there was so much building going on in Madison. There were one thousand buildings already and it was calculated there would be many more within the year. They were building in every nook and corner, on every lot in town. It only figured that with Madison the great western city, land in Burke would be certain to double and triple. With patience and hard work, they would be rich in the West. It was only a matter of time.

Nevertheless, Willard was happy with his new plow and his axe. He could subdue more land. That was what he dreamed of anyway. On the other hand, Ellen had to go back to living the way her ancestors had lived before 1800. Even back then the Spauldings had bought some "cake soap." Now Ellen had to rake up her hearth and put the ashes into the barrel outside for lye. With everything so high, she would have to make their soap.

Oh well, for Ellen there was one good thing — there were still quiltings out west. She had been invited to her first real quilting since coming out to Burke, and she was excited. Mrs. Cady was leaving, and she was having several quiltings to try to get all of her tops quilted before going to Iowa. All the neighbor women would be there at the brick house. And Ellen could feel pride knowing that she was a fine quilter, her stitches as small and straight and even as anybody's. The best thing of all, she could go alone. She did not need to beg Willard to take her. And it did not have to be on a Sunday either when Willard was forced to rest. He could be out in the thicket of oaks having another exciting day of swinging his axe, splitting another few hundred rails for his fencing. Ellen could put on her best dress, tie her bonnet strings, and pull that crude, wooden door behind her without even saying good-bye.

It was one week since Ellen last wrote to her parents, and she had lots of news to tell them.

Burke, Oct 27th, 1854.

Dear Mother,

I have taken my pen this morning, for the purpose of writing a few lines to you, for I allowed you would like to hear how we are getting along. We are both well, and fating up every day. Willard is fatter than he was last Spring, if he keeps on he will be a little Uncle Jep by and by, and I have grown poor so fast, that I do not weigh but a hundred and fifteen, and you need not be alarmed either, for it is all potatoe and butter fat, you never saw any one eat as we have since we came out here in your life, it keeps me half of the time almost cooking just for us, and if there was any more I should have to keep a maid for aught I know, and we do not begin with some of the neighbors, there was one of them here the other day, and he said it took six hundred lbs of pork for him, and his wife, and two little children, one a little biger than Austin, and the other just big enough to go alone. I got a letter from Leonora a few days ago, and a letter it was too, for she wrote some news, she gets more news than you do I guess. I was glad to hear she was better and the baby too and that the rest were all well, but Thomas and he was physicing off his visit I suppose and Esther she is having a hard time I should think with her visit. I guess if she gets over this and gets back home she will not go home again to stay very soon. I should think she would send for Lewis, if she has not. I got a letter from Mary Bagley last week. I guess she is home sick enoug that she will not be so crazy to go to Va again, if she gets home this time, she wrote she wanted to come home with Delorm²⁸ but she could not, for there she was, and there she had got to stay till Spring, good enough for her, and I guess Esther will say so too. I should think you are doing great business with the old maids this year. Leonora wrote Harison Keyes had married Nancy Parker, and I should like to know who she is, for I did not know any such Parker. I guess Mary Ann will go next. Has Hall Brewer gone home to take care of the old folks, if he has wont they shine? You wanted to know how I got along keeping house. I have got along well so far, and I shall get along better when we get moved and settled down and get something to do with. We went to Madison last Saturday and got a few things but they are so high here that our money and pork (for he could not sell but one hog) failed us before we had got many thing for keeping house and he must have some things to work with as well as I, and then his buying so much land and getting all over in debt but if you will come and live with us and Leonora can come out too that will do but if not

I shant think much of it. There is a farm here that Willard thinks Thomas could get if he wants it, it is on the same side of the road his Talcott farm is and goins it on the North, there is nothing but a log house on it and the house is about as far from our Cady house as from your house to the school house, and it is near school. Leonora wrote he talks of comeing out this Winter to look, but I should think he had better wait till Spring and take his family if he is comeing for it will cost a good deel for him to come and go back and then he could not tell any thing about the land in the Winter and I do not think but what he will like if he will come when it is warm and the ground is bare. It is very warm here now for the time of year. I raked up my fire soon as I got my breakfast out of the way and am sitting with the door open and am warm enough for comfort, and I suppose you are about getting out your sleighs. I have not been a visiting yet nor had company but once Mrs Cady came and spent one after noon and I have been and helped her quilt two afternoons she had a great quilting there was a lot of the neighbors there and some of them spoke to me and some went home without as much as saying why do you so (as Uncle Alden said [29]) I ex-pect they were affraid they should get bit. They have not so much as called any of them but Mrs Cady Mrs Ed-ward Talcott and Mrs Fitz Talcott. Edward Talcott has gone to Iowa to look but I hope he will not go there to live for they are good folks and I shall not want them to go away. Bradford Talcotts folks have not got back from Ohio yet. Georges folks are well I expect. I have not heard but they are. They have not taken pains enoug to come out and see us yet. Mr Haris and his wife [30] and one of the other girls went by one day but they did not dare to stop. I want you should write as soon as you get this and write all about every thing I want to know what you are doing about and what the neighbors find to talk about now I am gone. I want to know if you have seen or heard from Miriam Keyes and if Mary Fenn went to Boston as she talked of when I came away and I want to know what all the rest of the girls and boys are about and what Abner is going to do with himself this winter and write every thing else you can think of. I should like to take a look around there in town and I will some time and before many years too if you dont come out here to live but you will if you do not you will get a shaking when I get hold of you. We went to Madison last Saturday and traded about fifty dollars we got a stove for which we gave twenty seven dollars but we had some tin ware with it and we got some other things such as is necessary in a family and Willard got a plow and and an ax and we have got to go as soon as we can get time and get some more things for we have not got any thing yet hardly not any crockery nor wooden hosenture yet   50 dollars does not go far here getting things for they are so high, for there are so many people comeing to this country that they can ask just what they are a mind to and folks must have so they get their great prices which they would not if there was any other way to do, and they are plagued to get things any way, when Willard got our bed stead it was the only one there was in Madison and there was a number came and wanted to buy when he was there and had to go away without. You may give that white bonnet of mine to Leonora for the baby if she wants it, if you do not want it and my old dress that she wanted to make a comfortable of if you have not and she wants it, you know I was going to do all this business and a lot more but I came in such a hurry that I could not do nor think of any thing. as I am getting short of room, I shall have to close by bidding you good bye. write soon and write a good generous letter.

forever yours, Ellen E Reed,

Fortunately for Ellen, she only had to stay in the log cabin six weeks. The Cady family sold their property to Willard and left for Iowa so on Monday, October 30, Willard and Ellen moved up the hill into the Cady two-story, red-brick house.

For a short while Ellen was happier. Finally she had an acceptable house, one she did not have to be ashamed of when the ladies came to call. On the other hand, she had lost her neighbors and the items she had been borrowing from them. Making her situation much worse, three weeks after moving into the brick house, winter set in. Ellen and Willard quickly discovered they were going to freeze to death with only one little cast-iron stove inside this big, drafty house. Strange that Abner Cady, being their friend and an honest man, had not warned them. Certainly he had known that the house needed some work before another winter.

Two and one-half months in Wisconsin and, as far as Ellen could see, things were getting worse instead of better. Her only solution — she would appeal to her father for more money. What else could she do?

Burke   Nov 19ᵗʰ 1854

Dear Father and Mother,

Thinking perhaps you would like to hear from us again, I thought I would write a few lines. We are well, and hope these few lines will find you all the same. The snow that came last Sunday, all went off, and it has been quite warm, and the ground thawed out, so that Willard ploughed two days, but it is cold again today, and is snowing, and it looks like winter once more, but I hope it will not be cold long, for if it is I hardly know what we shall do, for Mr Talcotts folks have taken their things, and they, and Mr Edward Talcotts folks start for Iowa to morrow   We are left almost destitute of things   all we have is our stove and a little tin ware that we got with the stove, and a bed stead, a bed that we borrowed of Mr Todds folks and two plates of a Norwegean family and one old broken chair of Mrs Fitz Talcott, we cannot get things here as we could there for the neighbors have not got half enough for themselves. I forgot to tell

47

you that I have got a cace of 4 knives without any forks that Mrs Cady gave me when she went off. I have been looking every week for a letter with some money in it to get me some things with but have looked in vain. I do not know but you thought the $50 you sent me would get things enough for poor folks to get along with but it took more than half of it to get a stove with and that we must have to begin with and then there was some other little articles such as any family has to have to be got and Willard must have a plow or he could not plow the ground to raise any thing another year and it took it all without getting many things for me to do with, he would kill and sell his hogs and get some money to get some things with but pork is not but three dollars and a half per hundred and he does not want to sell for that as long as he has corn enough and every body thinks it will be up by and by to five or six per hundred and then I do not think it hardly belongs to him to buy me things for keeping house, and if you have got some money to spare, I wish you would send me some to get some things with as soon as you can. Willard is going to Madison again tomorrow to see if my box has come, he has got 8 lambs, he had a ten dollar bill on a broken bank and he let George Spaulding take it to trade off for him and he got the lambs for it, and George has got 20 more that Willard is going to winter for him. George has been quite sick with the jaundice, but is better *now, his oldest girl was married last Sunday and has gone to Madison to live, her man is a butcher. Mr Harrises folks have gone into their new house to live George sold for $1300 and is going to build a house on his farm and go to farming now, he calculates to take his money that he got for his tavern, and go to Iowa, and lay it out in land to speculate on. Willard has let his log house for a few months to a Mr Warren and I hope he is not so miserable as your Warren is as I do not think of any thing more to write now I will close. Write soon as you get this, and if you have any money for me, please send it soon as you can, for I want and need some things very much. We send our love to you all Forever yours, Ellen E Reed,*

Of course, Stedman immediately sent a check to Ellen and Willard, as well as the generous reply for them to get the things they needed and to send him the bill. Ellen had used strong words, "destitute of things...for poor folks to get along with...I want and need some things very much." [31]

Stedman had been there in Burke; he had seen the Cady brick house, Willard's log cabin. He had seen the land. He had met some of the people. Still he could not know for certain if his daughter's complaints were legitimate or if she simply was used to nice things and spoiled some. Besides, Willard was her husband now, and Stedman believed he should not interfere anymore than was necessary.

"We went to Madison last Tuesday and got some things, we had to get a table and bureau made, I will send a bill of the things soon," [32] wrote Willard on January 7, 1855.

Grayness, darkness, dreariness. All the land now was cast in somber shades of grays and browns with ominous clouds in the North, frosted-over ground, and skeletal oaks. The dried weeds that had been the brilliant wild flowers of the past summer were without shape, without color, dead. Everything here lay dormant, or waiting. There was a gray hush over the land. Cold and loneliness were ever with Ellen now, her constant companions to deal with hourly, one as hideous as the other, together utterly incapacitating – if it were not for the hope of spring and with it, Leonora's arrival.

But winter was not the only reason for Ellen's isolation and aloneness. She herself may not have realized yet that she was different from the women living nearby. They were all "tied up with babies." The care of children kept them continually busy. Most of what they thought or talked about related to their children. Ellen just did not fit in with them.

To fill some of the lonely hours, Ellen would get out her scrap bag. The pieces of Leonora's and her mother's new dresses, and of her grandma's apron may have cheered her as she pieced them into a block for her new quilt. These pieces of cloth were her proof that the world back east still existed. Leonora would already be wearing her dress. If Ellen were to journey through a long void, she would come to the other side where the silence would end; her loneliness would be obliterated immediately.

"After a long lonely winter,"[33] Ellen's hopes of Leonora ever living near her were dashed within just one innocent-looking letter. Instead of coming to the Western Country, Leonora's husband, Thomas Bagley, had moved his family to nearby Reading, Vermont.

Totally wrapped up in his own goals, Willard was not very sympathetic to Ellen. His wife's whining and crying had little effect on him when it came to his land. "I think Thomas was smart to go back to Reading, after being in such a strait to get away from there.[34] Ellen does not think much of it. she thinks there wont any body come now she has got out here, and is teaseing me to sell out and go back, but I do not want to do that, for this place suits me, and will make a splendid farm," he wrote back to Stedman. "There was a farm sold this winter, half a mile north, for three thousand, there was only eight acres more land than on this farm. it had but one advantage over this, and that was woods there was a bit of a framed house that cost about a hundred and fifty, a log house, and hog stable, forty acres broke, very poor fences, no hay marsh, nor stock water, I had rather have this farm by considerable," [35] Willard continued.

Not only was Ellen terribly disappointed over the news of Leonora, but after waiting six months, her box of things finally materialized at Mr. Pettegrew's in Madison. Where it had been, what its adventures had been, that was a real story. Had it been in six months of weather on top of stages, in uncovered wagons, in taverns and store rooms; or retrieved from a creek, stomped by horses, dumped to soak in various pots of dye, it could not have been in worse condition. It was a mockery of her parents' careful, concerned packing, the paper and cardboard all now mildewed into one soft, moldy, disintegrating heap, falling apart even as she handled it. It was a miracle the things were still inside, but no matter. As the shapeless mess seemed to melt open in Ellen's hands, horror upon horror fell to the plank floor. Everything was damaged.

Ellen had waited so long for her precious belongings — the beautiful heirloom linens and quilts she had spent so many hours tediously stitching, her stylish dresses, her card box. In the past she might not have appreciated them as much, but now Ellen was poor; these things had been her last nice possessions, her last remaining touch with the East and society. For the first time in her life she realized they could not be replaced; not as long as she was in the Western Country anyway.

Ellen continued writing at the end of the letter Willard had begun April 1, 1855. [36]

Dear Mother

As W,, has left a few lines I thought I would write a little. Spring has just made its appearance after a long lonely winter. I have been very lonely this winter but lived in hopes I should see Leonora but I have given up expecting to see any of my folks here to live now. I think it a shame to say so much to have us come and then all the rest stay behind but I do not care for if some of you do'nt come out and I do not feel any more contented I shall not stay long, perhaps you will blame me and say it is just as you expected, and if you do I cannot help it, there is beautiful land here and it is a pleasant place if I could have some company, but I have lived here all winter and not one of the neighbors has been into the house to take off hat or bonnet excepting Mr Talcotts folks till week before last the two Davis girls and their fellows came and made a visit. I have been down to Georges twice and Nathans twice and once to Mr. Harrises but Georges nor Nathans folks have not come near us any more than as if we were negroes. We have let a part of our hous to a family from N Y city they will stay this sumer and do not know but next winter, they have one child a little girl 5 years old so now I have some company. Georges folks have been out of the tavern a month so now they have no excuse for not coming but they cometh as they like about it but the Lord knows if my word is good that I shall not go there again if they are well till they have been here.

My things were badly damaged   my linnen was nearly all mildewed some and my silk dress spoiled entirely all but the waist and sleeves and the most of two bredths   my light lawn looked so bad that I would not have it in the house and I gave it to Mrs Talcott for her girl to wear every day and my berage delain was spotted bad and I sold it to Mrs Talcott and the rest will do for every day dresses, and my card box got wet and nearly spoiled and on the whole they were a hurd looking set but I could get along with that if I could have some company. I want you should be sure and come out next fall and stay a good while and see if you like well enough to come out and live and if you dont I shall not stay here any longer than till he can sell reasonably, and we will try and find a place somewhere, where we can have some company for I think there is such places in the world. I do not think of any thing more to write   only blame me if you are a mind to, write soon as you get this (for I want to hear from you very much   it is all the company I have) and write about every body and every thing for I want to hear from all.

(This is a piece of W,s, shirts)   my love to all
                                        Forever yours
                                          Ellen

Spring finally came to Burke and with it, renewed hope for Ellen for she promised herself that it would not always be so lonely — her parents would be out in a year or two. Then she could have some company. For now, Ellen looked forward to their trip to see Albert's folks, people she had known back home.

One week later...

Burke, Monday April 9th 1855.

Dear Father & Mother

I write a few lines this morning to let you know that yours of the 25th was received with pleasure, we are always so glad to hear from you and the rest of our friends. I was very glad to hear you was all well. We are well as usual, and hope these lines will find you the same. I am puttering around as usual. Willard has been fixing fenceing stuf till now he is going to geting his land ready, for sowing his wheat, and I shall be glad when the crops are in the ground for then we are going down to see Alberts folks and it will seem good to me to see one face that I used to see when I was at home for I have not yet since I came out. Georges folks were here yestoday, they are all well, and getting their house done fast as they can calculate to get so as to move into it in June if they can, they are now living with Mr Harris. Willard has gone to get a kettle to make soap, Mrs. Talcott and I are going to make together. You thought I should not get my soap made so easy as L., has, but I would not care for the

54

soap if I was where I could see you as she can but never mind it will not always be as it is now for I expect you will come out here to live in a year or two   if not I do not think I shall stay. I want you should be sure and come out next fall and see us. I should think Esther would be tired waiting for Lewis to come home   I should think he would if he knew how unwell she is. I wish she would come and stay with me this summer, where is Mary and her man going to live probably in some large city. tell Ivory[37] that I want he should write to me if he knows he has got any such cousin out here, and tell Stoughton to write too and all the rest to write and not wait for me to write to each one seperate   when I write to one it is to all. I have not heard from Miriam yet   I expect she has forgoten me entirely. tell Mary (Bagley) that I am waiting as patiently as I can to get an answer from a letter I sent her a long time ago, I do not know but she has got above writing to me now since it is Mrs Williams but I hope it is not the case with you all, how I wish I could see you all. You may tell Leonora that I am as mad as a hoe because she did not come out here. tell her she has lost her silk dres for Oella for if she had come out I should have given her one   there is enough in mine that is good to make her one when she gets big enough to go alone. there is a little snow left yet but it will not last many days for it is quite warm here now, it has been a very hard winter for this country. You wanted to know which place I had rather winter in, it is a great deal colder here, then there and if there was not so much snow there I should rather winter there and if the Lord spares my life perhaps I shall before many years have passed, that is if you want I should, for I have no notion of living out here alone many years   I have had all the dried apples I wanted, they are 12 1/2 cents a pound and almost every thing is a great deal higher here than there. I am in a great hury for Mr Howard[38] is almost ready so I must close. I wrote to you last sunday so I have not much news to write only we have got a pair of geese.   now be sure and come this fall and perhaps we can make you twice glad. give my love to all write soon and often for paper and ink is cheap.

Tell Mrs Riggs[39] that I have not forgotten her, the reason I do not write but I write to you so often that I do not get any thing new to write and you my let her read your letter if you are a mind to   I should like to have her write to me very much and I will try and write to her. You may read this to her but dont let her see it nor any body else for it looks so bad   give my love to her and every body else that inquires for me

Ellen had all the fixings to do for the trip to Union to the Adams the first weekend in May. Willard borrowed George Spaulding's nice new buggy, and they had a "first rate good visit"[40] seeing familiar faces from Ludlow. With so many friends and such a large family,

Ellen probably never would have thought she could be so happy to see Albert Adams and his wife, or folks who had been nearly strangers back in Vermont. But it was wonderful to have "back home" to gossip and reminisce about. All too soon, Willard was hitching up the horse to the buggy, and they were heading north again to Burke.

One month later...

Burk June 8th 1855.

Dear Father & Mother

I have taken my pen in hand once more to write a few lines to you to let you know that yours of May 27th was gladly received, we were very glad to hear from you and hear you was all well, and I hope these lines will find you the same. We are in comfortable health now, although I have been quite sick. We went down to Union and had a first rate good visit but when we come home it was a cold windy day and I took a hard cold which laid me on my back one week under the Doctors care. I had a little run of the bilious fever, and when I got better of that I commenced coughing, which has proved to be the hooping cough and Willard has got it too but you need not have a fit about it now for we are both getting better. Willard is having it very light and I should probably if I had not taken a hard cold but it is a good time of year and I am very glad that we have got along so far so well with it and now we shall not have that to think about. I have given it to some eight or ten about here, before we knew

what it was, now dont you wory about us, for we are
doing well, and if you do I wo'nt write to you next time,
and if you do, I shall find it out. I did not have any
luck at all with my goslins   there did not but one hatch
and that died for want of breath. I have got 26 turkeys
and three more turkeys to hatch, have no chickens yet but
hope to have some by & by, have got five little pigs, and
four old ones. the cow Willard bought last fall has not
calved yet, but he has bought another that gives milk so I
have milk and make butter to sell. I have been to the city
today and carried six pounds of (good) butter but it is not
but 12 1/2 cts a pound here and it seems almost like giving
it away   he gave 31 dollars for his cow, stock is very high
here. The mans name is Howard that lives in the house
with us and is a machinest by trade, and the mans name
that lives in the log house is Robins and they are good
folks too. You wrote that you thought of comeing out this
fall but if you did not calculate to stay only for a visit, I
had rather you would wait till spring and then sell or let
your farm and come and stay a year at least and then you
would not go back I guess to stop long. Willard talks of
going up north about a hundred miles, to the pinery to get
out lumber this winter and if he does I though I should
come home and stay with you this winter if you wanted
me to and would come back with me in the spring, there
is a Mr Clark that married one of Uncle Levis girls down

to Union and he is going back after his wife this fall and I can go with him and feel safe. I got a letter from Ester a few days ago, she wrote she was expecting L at home this month and I hope he will come for her sake and then I shall expect to see them out here. I got a letter from Maria a few days ago, they were all well when she wrote. I got a new parasol yestoday, and I bought a new dress of the woman that lives here, that was 25 cts a yard, and I will send you a piece. I do not think of much more this time, and I must leave the rest of the room for W, or he will be a whining, so I must close once more, write as soon as you get this for I want to know what you think about comeing back with me in the spring. good by for now, my love to all, ever your Ellen

Five weeks later, Ellen wrote to her parents at the end of a letter Willard had started.

Burke July 15th 1855

As Willard has left room for me I suppose I must write but I hardly know what for we do not get much news. My health is good as usual but not any better than it used to be there, but I am in hopes when I get entirely over the hooping cough that I shall be healthier. I was very sory to hear your health is so poor this summer, but I hope it will be better, if not I think you had better try and come out here to winter for the winters are not so long and hard here as there and I do not think but what some of the rest will take Grandsire [41] I should give them a chance at any rate. When you write I want to know how Uncle Aldens folks do, and how things go on at Uncle Wymans, [42] I suppose about after the old sort I wonder what the reason is that you do not send me yours and Grandsirs & Grandmas [43] deguaerreotypes and Ivory says he left his and Stoughtons there to send to me but I have not seen them yet. You wanted to know about my cellar, it is a very good one what there is of it, it is only under one room Willard has fixed me a cupboard to put my milk in and a table to skim it on

I have not seen Uncle Levis folks but I should like to first rate but there is not many folks from the east that finds where we are. Ivory happened too, but I almost wonder how he happened to I shall expect to see Lewis Clines folks here when he gets home if he ever does. I suppose you had a great time there the 4th a couple cents worth of fire works or some thing of that kind as usual, there was a circus in Madison and all most all the neighbors went but us and we thought it would not pay. I do not know whether I have ever sent you a piece of my dress or not if I have no matter, and if not I will, I do not think of much more to write now I want you should write as soon as you get this and not wait a month as you did be fore and write abut all the young folks and old ones to, give my love to Grandma and Grandsire and tell them that I should like to see them out here this fall and you had better come and stay this winter. remember me to all the rest of the folks that I should like to see. It is night and I must close so good by for this time, write soon and not wait. Yours forever and aye,

Ellen E Reed

No longer did Ellen have hours of time on her hands. Her cousin Ivory Haven somehow had shown up on their doorstep in Burke and now lived with them, so Ellen had his washings to do and another mouth to feed. And Willard's land was being transformed into a busy farm with life squawking and scampering all about underfoot, most of it Ellen's responsibility. Besides all of that, Ellen had agreed to put her butter into jars and to carry it to the city to sell.

One month since her last letter home...

Burke, August, 13th, 1855.

Dear Father & Mother,

I am not agoing to do by you as you did by me, wait a month before I answer yours of July 29th. I got almost out of patience waiting for a letter I should think as I am all the one you have to write to that you might write a little oftener. I was very glad to hear your health was improving and hope it will continue too till you are well again, for there is nothing like good health and without it any one cannot enjoy themselves let them be where they will. I am gaining some and hope I shall get entirely over my cough before cold weather, with the exceptions of that we are all well and hope these lines will find you the same. Ivory is with us yet. Willard has got some hay cut and is now cutting more on the marsh, he has got his wheat all in the barn and his oats, he has taken a few acres of oats and has got them to cut yet, his corn is ten feet high now and growing every day, we have had new corn for several days and new potatos for two weeks, and you may tell Mr Lamb I had ripe tomatoes last week, we are not going to have any cucumbers this year, and not many mellons, our plumb trees have got a few plums on them, they never bore before. The woolvs caught all of my turkeys but one. I wrote to Leonora a great while ago but she has not answered it yet I expect she has forgoten me entirely, she has got so many brothers and sisters to write to that I suppose I ought not to expect a letter very often. I should think Esther would begin to think that Lewis was never comeing home. We got a letter from Maria a few days ago, and one from Charles, he is working at home this summer with his Father on the old place, but he thinks it is the last summer he shall work there for he calculates to come out West in the spring, but you may keep still and say nothing about it to any one, they was all well there when they wrote. George is to work

Maria L. Reed, J. Willard Reed's half sister.
Photograph courtesy of George Adams Parkhurst.

for one of their neighbors this summer. The folks that lives in the log house and the folks that live in this house are going to start next thursday for their land in Richland Co. and I shall be glad, for they have proved to be real mean New Yorkers, they will take what ever they want where ever they can find it and they have had a tribe of hens and geese and turkeys and pigs a ransacking around the house and barn about as long as we care about them. I wish you would come out and stay this winter but I dont suppose you will, for if you dont think enough of me to write more than once a year, it is not likely you would be to the expense of comeing so far to see me, but that does not make but what I should be glad to see you. I hope you will answer this a little sooner than you did the other one. I am going to send one to Grand ma in this. I do not think of any thing more to write this time so I will bid you good bye once more. We are takeing the Madison paper this year and are agoing to send them to you, we have got some papers from you and shall be glad to get more any time, we all send our love to you one and all great and small.

This from your affectionate daughter _Ellen E Reed_

One week later, Ellen again filled the rest of the sheet of Willard's letter, dated August 21, 1855.

Dear Mother,

As I have room I will write a few lines. I wrote last that I was going to Madison in a few days. I did go and cary my butter, and sold it to Mr Fullers folks for 16 cts and they wanted I should put them down a jar full of my poor butter for winter. Mrs Fuller had been quite sick but was better then. The folks that lived with us and in the log house have all gone, and good ridance to bad rubage. I got a letter from Leonora last week, and was glad to hear such good news all around among them. I can not stop to write any more for I am going to washing, so good bye, write soon, Yours, Ellen

One month later, the rains, humidity, and heat had ended. The wheat was ready, the threshers came, fall had arrived.

Burke Sep 25th [1855]

Dear Father & Mother,

I have taken my pen once more for the purpose of writing a few lines to you, to let you know that your last letter was gladly received, and was glad to hear you was all well. We are well as usual and hope these lines will find you the same, perhaps you are thinking the time long to wait for a letter, but you will excuse us when you hear the business of the past week. Willard had his threshing done last Friday and Saturday and that you know made work for him and me too [44] *his wheat did not turn out as well as it did last year, he had 200. bushels and as many oats he carried a load of wheat to Madison yestoday and got $1 '20 per bushel and contracted all he could draw today and tomorrow for the same, wheat is considerable higher than it was last year at this time, oats are 40 & 50 cts a bushel, and that is very high for this country, and all kinds of groceries are very high and I do not know but they are every where the same, we can not get any thing in the shape of sugar short of 9 and 10 cts, butter is 18 & 20 cts now in Madison. Willard has got some of his corn cut up, he let Talcott have that land for 20 dollars per acre, and he pays part this fall and part next fall and the rest the next fall* and he is a going to furnish lumber and finish the house for us this fall. it was very rainy here all last week and it rained some yestoday. I am footing a pair of stockings for myself now, I have cut a plain waisted dress for Mrs Talcott and got a first rate fit too, and have made Willard a pair of pants and he fetched home cloth for another pair last night, so you see I am jack at all traids. I think your calico of your comfortable is very prety and that card too that you sent me. I suppose you are fixing your things to come out here you had better be at any rate. I shall expect you out in the spring, and stay all summer. Georges folks have got into their new house, they are all well or was the last I knew of them, and Nathans folks was well all but one of the girls her health is very poor this summer and Nathan told me a few weeks ago that they was affraid she was going in the consumption. I have not heard much about the cholera this year not half as much as I used to there, there is quite a number around now sick with a fever. I do not think of any thing more to write now and am in a hury for I am going to wash to day so I will close my short letter and write more next time. write soon as you get this for we want to hear from you.

Ivory is driving stage from Madison to Portage,[45] and I do his washings for him, (that is all), so good bye for now

Yours in haste

Ellen,

Only several weeks later, Ellen was so proud and happy. She wasn't lonely either, for now she had her hands full. She had a helper too. Perhaps because Ellen was family, Mary and George Spaulding had suggested she and Willard take eight-year-old Adelle to raise as their own. Mary's sister was on her way to California to find her husband. There was no way she thought she could take her child with her. Heartbreaking as it was to everyone involved, she had made the decision that Adelle must stay behind there at Token Creek. Actually, Mary and George believed Adelle was an orphan now (people going out to the gold country never seemed to return). They were too old to give the child what she needed — young parents like her own. And Mary and George were probably aware of Ellen's loneliness. Ellen did not seem to be able to have a child of her own — she had been married over one year already and still she was childless. Ellen and Willard's parenting her had appeared to be the most sensible solution. Ellen needed Adelle, and the abandoned child certainly needed a mother.

Burke   Oct 21ˢᵗ 1855

Dear Father & Mother

I take my pen once more for the purpose of writing a few lines to you, to let you know that yours of Oct 7ᵗʰ, was gladly received, we was very glad to hear that you was all well, and hope these lines will find you the same. We are well as usual. I suppose you want to know what we are about here, well I will tell you. Willard has got his corn into the barn but has not husked much yet, he has got part of his plowing done, he has sold all of his wheat for one dollar and twenty cts a bushel, but since then it has been a dollar and a half   wheat has been very high here this year. It has been very pleasant weather the most of the time this fall with the exception of two snow storms, it snowed here week before last, and it snowed again last night a little. I have cut and made Willard a pair of pants, and made me a dress, and I will send you a piece, I think that of your comfortable is very prety   I should think you was fixing a lot, and when you get your fixing done I hope you will come out here. I think the folks there must be smart to all stop to Union to live for it is no better place than it is here. I want you should have Grandma and Grandpa to have their daguaerreotypes taken and send with yours and Ivory said he and Stoughton left theirs there last fall to send so you may put them in too and as many more as you can get, and we will have ours taken and send to you the first chance we have. Perhaps you did not know we have got a little girl to our house, well we have, and one that is not to be sneered at too, and now I suppose you will want to know what the name is, it is Adelle, now dont that beat Oella, all to nothing. Georges folks are all well, Mr Harris has sold his land and house, and is going to moove in with Georges folks now, Nathans folks are well or was the last I heard from them   their son Albert was married last Sunday, and the two Davis girls that live in this neighborhood was married a week ago last Thursday. It has been very sickly about here this summer and fall so far but now it is comeing on cold weather I hope it will be healthier. Willard is writting to George[46]

68

today   I have not heard a word from Esther since I, got home and I think it quite strange. I am expecting a letter from Leonora soon if she has not forgoten me and I hope not for I wrote her a long time ago, and then I hope I shall hear from E. I do not think of any thing more worth writing so I will close. I want you should write as soon as you get this. our love to all, good bye,   yours, Ellen,

   (give one piece to Grandma)

Oh I forgot to tell you our girl is one that we have taken if her mother dont come and and take her and she is in California so there is not much danger   she is 8 years old and her mother is sister to George Spauldings wife.[47]

Another month passed. Only Willard wrote to Stedman and Arterista.

Burke Nov 25th, 1855

Dear Father & Mother

        I write a few lines to let you know that yours of the 12th was received. We were very glad to hear from you for we had been waiting a long time for a letter. we are well and hope the same from you. we have had fine weather here all the fall untill a week ago, when we had about three inches of snow. since that it has been rather cold and windy.   I have been hoping for a week more of plowing weather, but I think it is rather doubtful. I cannot complain for there was but one day up to the 16th that the ground was froze enough to prevent plowing. I worked a month at it and did not miss but three days. I have taken 24 acres of land adjoining the Talcott farm to put into wheat next year on shares, and have got it nearly all plowed. besides that I have plowed eight acres at home. every thing that farmers raise is high this fall, and I have had a little of most every thing to sell. I have paid for the cow that I bought last Spring, have paid George forty dollars, my threshing bill which was seventeen dollars. I have had to get trusted for Store goods since last winter, and for all my farming tools, and have got the most of it paid up. the state interest money, and taxes are behind yet, but I have got a few oats, and a fat cow, (with the exception of one quarter) to sell yet. I traded off my oxen yesterday for a span of horses. they are good heavy horses kind and true, one is eight and the other is nine. I intend to team with them on the road some this winter. there is a vast amount of teaming done here from the railroad into the country north from here. they pay fifty cents a hundred for hauling from Madison to Portage. a good team will take up from 20 to 24 hundred, and most always get a load back either grain or lumber. a team can make the trip in four days easy. I should like to know if you want any money this winter. I have made well this summer and am about square for little debts, and now the next thing is to pay big ones. I have got my horses, three cows that are coming in in the spring, a yearling and two calves, and all that I owe for them is five dollars. I am tough as a bear. Ellen says that, she and I, eat more than all four of us did when we was at home. She baked a huge loaf of brown bread the other afternoon, and thought she had got bread enough to last a day or two, but I came in at night from ploughing and we sat down and eat most every mouthful of it, and meat & potatoes accordingly. as I do not think of any thing more I must close (write soon)

Yours J. W. Reed

(I forgot to mention)

Ellen wrode out horse back to day, and she thinks if grandma Haven sends out her side saddle she shall be able to go out on the prairie after the cows next summer.

It was an amazing thing — last year this time Ellen had felt miserable; now it was winter again, the coldest weather ever known there, yet strangely enough, Ellen was enjoying herself. Even her sore throat and side were better as long as she stayed warm. This winter she and Adelle were cooking so much that Ellen thought she was as fat as she ever was. And Willard had such an appetite that he ate "most everything" she could make.

Ellen seemed to have more energy too. The winter before she had accomplished so little, but this winter she spent every extra moment sewing. She had made a pair of shirts for Ivory, a pair of pants for Willard, new dresses for Adelle and herself, and she was piecing a new comfortable. Keeping her company, Adelle may have been at Ellen's side with a needle and thread learning to piece a simple four-patch block from the scraps Ellen had left over.

Ellen may have even begun thinking that Burke would be fine after all, when one day in February Willard announced that he had sold most of their Cady farm. Just that fast, Ellen and he were moving. Whatever Ellen's feelings were, she had no choice but to continue the tradition of the great western lie: never let them know the truth back east. Only write how good it was. Certainly she did want others to come.

Two and one-half months since his last letter, Willard wrote to Stedman and Arterista. Ellen penned a note at the top of the page:

I should like to know what has become of Mary Bagley, she has got so smart since she is Mrs Williams that she can not write to little folks, but let her go ahead   great things burst sometimes.

Burke Feb 3ᵈ 1856

Dear Father & Mother
    I write a few lines to let you know that we are well, and that yours of the 20ᵗʰ was received. we are having the coldest weather ever known. there has been but two days since the 20ᵗʰ of Dec warm enough to thaw on the south side of buildings. the 8ᵗʰ of Jan the thermom-eters about here stood at 38 degrees below zero, but it has been hard telling when the coldest was. it has been all cold. we hear of some one being frozen to death every day or two, but we have had no snow for sleighing. I went across the marsh Friday after a load of wood and came near freezing my fingers. yesterday I froze my ears & nose just doing

the chores. to day is a trifle warmer. I have just had a
letter from Charles Reed I expect him out the first of
march. he wanted to know if there is any money for him
at Ludlow. I told him that I supposed there was some
for him when he was of age, and that I thougt it would
not make any difference if he had it a month or two before
that time, and to be sure and come through Ludlow. I
wish you would write to him about it soon as you get this.
I can let him have the money on your account if you wish
me to. if so you can give him an order for it, and send me
the receipt for him to sign. I have sold out the Cady farm
I sold for thirty dollars an acre. I have $500. in the
Spring, and $200. a year at seven per cent, and have
security on the land. this with what I get from Talcott
makes $600. more than I gave. I shall sell the rest if
I get what I ask. I have refused $1500. for it. my
price is $1800. I am certain that I can do better to sell
and buy a lot of government land. I want to take a look
around in the Spring and see the country. there are several at the "Creek" going to Adams Co in the Spring.
Harris has bought 400 acres there. The advantages for
timber & water are much better in that section than here. we
are going to live in Wm,, Adams, house this summer. his
is the new house that you saw on opposite side of Talcott,s.
If I sell the rest of my land in the Spring I can let
you have some money if you wish. if not I shall lay it

out in land again. I wish that I could send you some of our nice flour. I went to the Madison mill the other day, and carried about twelve bushels of wheat, corn & buckwheat. I got over 3/4 of a barrel of flour from four bushels of wheat. as I do not think of anything more I must close.   I remain yours
                    J. W. Reed

Ellen continued writing on the back of the letter.

Monday morning

You wanted I should write about my throat and side, they do not trouble me now only when I get cold so I call them well now, my health has not been any better for four years than it is now and I am as fat as ever I was, and Willard is tough as a knot and you never saw him near as fat as he is now. Adelle is here yet   she is a very good little girl and we like her very well so far. she is very willing to help me all she can and I never have to ask her the second time to do any thing   she is going to school now. Ivory was here yestoday, he is well and enjoying himself first rate this winter   he is driving stage yet. I do his washing but shall not much longer if we moove down to Bills (as we call him) I expect he will board with us and then when Charles comes I shall have enough to do without takeing in washing. I have made Ivory a pair *of shirts this winter and. I will send Grandma a piece of them   I wish she or you or both would come out with Charles and you shall have company back when you get ready to go. I have got Adelle a new dress and she wants I should send you a piece, she is lotting on going East with us, but not half as much as I am. I want you should write soon and write all about the boys and girls and where Delorm is   I have not heard a word about him in a long time   he has not left this world and entered the great state of matrimony   has he*

Ellen E Reed,

Six weeks later, Willard had already "been up north to see the country." [48] He had taken a load from Madison about a hundred miles up to Stephens Point for one of the merchants, bought a light load of shingles, and then brought it back. He returned to Burke excited at the great home market for all that could be raised up north due to the booming lumbering business. Still he wanted to look around before he bought. "If I sell the rest of my land," he wrote to Stedman, "I shall go out into Iowa and Minesota and see where I like best, and where there are the best chances for timber & water, and to make improvements. I want to get government land if I can find a choice location. if not I shall buy second handed land." [49]

Ellen continued Willard's letter.

March 19th

Willard has wrote most all he can think of so I thought I would try and help him some. It is very warm and pleasant for the time of year, the roads are dry and dusty. I have been almost sick this week I have got a bad cold but that is not the worst trouble, last monday the Dentist come and pulled three teeth and filled six more,[50] *and now I guess you will not wonder at my not feeling very smart. you need not think I had the teeth ache so bad that I had them drawn for they did not ache a speck but were very rotten, (no I have not come to the teeth ache yet) We are expecting Charley every day. There was a man here yestoday to look of the land, and I hope he will take it, for we want to be off somewhere, where there is wood and water. I think it is a great idea that I cannot get a letter from Esther. I have wrote to her twice, and received no answer, and next time I shall send the letter to you, and see if you can send it to her We have given up expecting you out here and I do not know when we shall come there. I think Grandmas dress is very pretty. when you write I wish you would send me a lot of patterns for working skirts and pantiletts I have got a girl now that has to be worked around the edges you know. I am pieceing me a comfortable, called Boneparts retreat.*[51] *Mrs Harris has got another baby. babies are as thick out here as flies in the sumer, but poor folks like us cannot afford it.*

Month after month Ellen scrubbed her rags in her tub of boiling water. Each month the water grew crimson — another month gone by and still she was not in a family way. Her sister, Leonora, had no trouble becoming pregnant, but she suffered weeks each time

recovering from the delivery. When her niece was born, Ellen may even have been in that stuffy, hot, darkened birthing room to comfort her sister, maybe to hold her hand. Certainly Ellen knew of the possible perils of childbirth; yet she also accepted that as a woman's lot. She would be a failure as a wife if she could not give Willard children. After a year and a half without success, Ellen had to save face — she had to give an explanation even to her parents, an excuse to herself, that they simply could not afford to have a baby.

Ellen should have known she would be moving sooner than calculated. That was Willard's way. Two weeks later Willard drew up a land agreement with a Myron Lyon for $1500 for the northeast corner of Section 24, nearly one hundred miles northwest, in a place called Glendale Township, Wisconsin. It was second-handed land after all — but only on paper. Lyon was a speculator. Intending to sell at a profit, he had bought numerous acres of government land when it came onto the market the year before. And Mr. Lyon was *so nice*. He made it easy for Willard to buy, only a little money down, and he was not in any hurry for the rest. That was an offer that Willard could not resist. Had he taken time to go to Iowa or Minnesota to look, Lyon's land might be sold, so he grabbed it quickly. Besides, it was a choice location — about equally divided into "perrarie," woodland, and marsh with the

Baraboo River running right through the center.

At least they would not be all alone there, Ellen could console herself, for Leonora's sister-in-law and husband, Esther and Lewis Cline, were making final arrangements to come out and buy some of the land from Willard. In Glendale Township, Ellen would have Esther right next door. So Ellen worked everyday fixing her things to move. Willard would have to make several loads. The rest of their goods and his yoke of steers he could leave with the Talcotts until the following spring.

Tragically for Ellen, she had to give Adelle back to the Spauldings at Token Creek. Ellen never wrote another word about her little girl. Knowing Willard's cool practicality, most likely he had decided that times would be hard and that the rough Wisconsin wilderness was no place for an eight-year-old girl. Besides, it would be many months before they would have a place of their own to live. Until then they would have to make do the best they could living with other settlers. Best that Adelle go back to Token Creek with her aunt and uncle George and Mary Spaulding. And just that fast, Ellen lost her little girl.

It would seem Ellen could not talk about it; only Willard wrote the next letter home.

Glendale, April 26ᵗʰ 1856

Dear Father & Mother

I write a few lines to ask your pardon for our neglect in writing and let you know that we are alive and kicking. Stoughton is with us. I have not seen Ivory since I left Burke I was down there when the boys came there and I came up with, and Ivory went to Fall

River.   he has probably got into work before now.   we received a letter from Lucian to day. the folks were all well. we have received three letters from Esther. they wrote that they were going to start west as soon as they received a letter from us, so that they might know where to come to.   I answered their first letter too months ago. it seems curious that they should not know where we live. If you see anybody that wants to find us, tell them we are in Town 15 North of range 1 East, on Section 24. the Spring is very backward   folks about here began to plough yesterday for the first time. last night it rained all night, and it has snowed all day. when you answer this I should like to have you write what you think about coming out this fall. There seems to be a general complaint of hard times throughout the country, provisions are scarce and high. I sold twelve bushuls of potatoes the other day for as good as ten dollars (I got seven hundred feet of fine flooring,) and have got some more to spare. I want to get my house so we can get into it by the middle of June. our farm is about equaly divided into perrarie, woodland, and marsh. we have got a nice building spot. it is on the east side of the woods about ten rods from the river. as I do not think of anything more I must close by biding you good bye

I remain yours

,,write soon,,   J. Willard Reed

79

Willard was one of the first to buy land and settle in Glendale (it had just come onto the market in 1855). Unfortunately for him in the future, he had not bought his land directly from the government but from a land speculator whose family had quickly grabbed up much of the township when the land had first come onto the market.

In 1856, when Ellen and Willard arrived, there were very few settlers in the entire Baraboo Valley. The only glimmer of civilization was the Fowler Settlement, two miles down the old Indian trail from Willard's new land. Three brothers and their families, Reuben, John, and Merril Fowler had come in 1851 and made their own small community. Each of them had built a log house on his farm, and together they had put up the Fowler School the following year. By 1856, the Fowlers were well established and nearly self-sufficient. They were good, hospitable people, taking in the new settlers until they could find other accommodations. So it was when Ellen and Willard arrived — the Reuben Fowler family took them in.

But what was Ellen to do from morning till night out there in the wilderness with only a tiny room in someone else's log house? She no longer had a little girl "to work around the edges" and to keep her company either. Willard had months of back-breaking toil ahead of him. He had to start from the beginning once again clearing, breaking, grubbing his densely wooded, virgin land, then building a log house, splitting and putting up rail fences, plowing, and planting. He would be working from morning till night everyday now for months. There was no time, nor provisions, for his none-too-well, whining wife. Most likely with Ellen's insistence, the decision was made that she should go back to Ludlow, Vermont, and stay with her parents until Willard was able to get into their own place. Willard made arrangements for her to go back with someone traveling in that direction and soon Ellen was on her long-awaited journey home.

After the endless hours of passing through prairies, forests, farmland, then the oblivion of nighttime, more farmland and woods, the train was finally leaving Albany, then Schenectady. In about four more hours they would be in Rutland, Vermont. In only a few more, Ellen would be home. The landscape was changing to the beauty and serenity of New England. There was pride in every white clapboard and shuttered house; pride in every plowed and planted field; the glistening white church with spire crowning each village with grace and peace. Ellen was a proud Vermonter no matter how long she lived in Wisconsin. Her roots were in Vermont, forever.

One can only imagine Ellen's homecoming: the tears of joy, the arms entwined, the tender hugs, the laughter, the warmth and love Ellen had not felt since she had left Vermont nearly two years earlier. What an incredible change of settings from being out in the sparsely settled, silent wilderness, to the bustling, gregarious, populated village of Ludlow, Vermont. Ellen must have been overwhelmed with happiness. In Reading with Leonora and the three little ones, she spent many light-hearted days gossiping, giggling, saying things she could tell only her sister. And comforting hours sped by bent over Grandma Haven's quilting frame, pushing and pulling the gently curved-from-use needle through the layers of Grandmother's most recent creation. The majority of time, however, Ellen spent at home with her parents. At times she may have forgotten her problems; she may have had moments when she felt carefree as in her youth, but now she had a new worry — her back and sides ached and her cough would not go away.

The days sped by so quickly. It was past her intended time of return to Wisconsin; in fact, six months had elapsed. Willard was waiting. So, about the first of December, Ellen had to prepare to return to that isolated, dreary valley in Wisconsin. No matter, her first responsibilities were as Willard's wife. As much as she must have dreaded leaving her mother, her father, her pregnant sister (not to mention her niece and nephews, cousins, grandparents, and friends), she simply had no choice. "For richer, for poorer, in sickness and in health, till death do us part...," those were the vows she had made. Ellen had known the day would come when she would have to say good-bye, when she again would be on the cars, this time the train pushing farther and farther *away* from her beloved Vermont and painfully slowly toward her lonely plight in the West.

The train began jerking, heaving forward. The depot passed her window, arms waving handkerchiefs, splashes of somber hues of quilted bonnets and wools. Then they were gone. She was once again moving from the safety, security, and abundance of New England to her gloomy, desolate, lean western existence.

The train wound its way along ledges of mountains of dark, green-blue pine, spruce, maple, and ash; down into valleys following gushing, crystal-clear blue rivers and brooks; past mills and villages and white spires, into bright clearings of well-kept farms and neat midwestern towns, over wooded hills and onto prairies. New York, Pennsylvania, Ohio, Indiana, Illinois. After a seemingly endless journey, the train reached Chicago. Willard would already be in Burke preparing to meet the train when it arrived at the Madison depot.

On December 5, 1856, Ellen walked off the cars by the station platform at Madison, Wisconsin. Willard was there to meet his wife. It was freezing cold; Ellen was coughing, but she had to ride almost ten miles in an open rig to William Adams's new frame house on the quarter section below their first cabin in Burke. There Ellen and Willard stayed for a short while with their former neighbors. Then they moved into the Talcotts' two-story log house across the road.

It was Willard who wrote to Vermont of Ellen's safe return.

Burke, Dec 7th 1856

Dear Father & Mother,

I write a few lines to let you know that Ellen arrived here day before yesterday safe and well as could be expected. George is here,[52] though I expect he will leave tomorrow. Ellens things all came through safe and sound. I am stoping with Wm Adams he lives in the new framed on the opposite side of the road from Talcots. I am going up north in a few weeks. I have got two yoke of oxen and four cows & 3 yearlings here. Talcot is going up with me to look, and if he likes is going to buy there. I want to get up there and get out a lot of fencing, and build a house and some log stables. the man that I bought of went away last Spring and did not come back untill Fall I began to think he was not coming back and I carried the money in my pocket long enough to wear it out, and so I bought another small place, of 130 acres for $900 and paid nearly all down and when the man came back he wanted me to keep the land and gave me four years to pay for it,[53] and I liked the land and got it so cheap I would keep it. some folks say it is the best farm in the Barraboo valley. I was in hopes Charles would have come out and bought half of it. I am going to draw a plan of it and send it to you soon. it is well timbered, and watered with four creeks and four Springs, and has plenty of good hay marsh. I have got twenty five acres broke and *seventeen fenced. the La Cross rail road is coming within nine miles of it, and will probably be completed within a year, but I must now close. my health is good, I am tough and hearty, but I think Ellen looks as if the climate of Vermont did not agree with her, but I will write no more give my love to all*

(write soon)

yours truly

J. W. Reed

Abruptly, Ellen had returned to a man's world, to the talk of wood and water, corn and wheat, fences and barns. After journeying days to see her husband, the conversation was only about new land, more debt, more elaborate arrangements to get rich in the West. Furthermore, Ellen had only arrived when Willard must have informed her that he and Talcott were going to Glendale to look around, that she would be staying with Mrs. Talcott several weeks. Only after that would they be returning to Glendale together.

Willard had no way of knowing of the terrible cold spell ahead. It was dangerously cold up north. At times the roads were completely gone; only mountains of snow covered everything like the wilderness again as if man had never been, his years of toil hidden under seas of immobilizing whiteness. For Ellen and Elnira Talcott, isolated in the log house in Burke, the days stretched into hours, then to minutes, even seconds as they nervously waited. Without any way of communication, the imagination could conjure up all kinds of horrors. If Willard had been on his way back when the storm hit — and surely he was for all the calculations made — then he may have lost his way, maybe even lie buried, frozen somewhere. Doubtless, Ellen and Elnira were very happy to see their husbands when they finally returned home.

It was nearly two months after Ellen's return from Vermont, on January 28, 1857, that she and Willard could finally leave the

Talcotts to begin their trip back to Glendale — a journey of seventy-five miles in an uncomfortable, open wagon.

Mrs. Talcott returned a letter to Ellen's mother on February 12:

Mrs. Spaulding

your kind letter was brought to me this evening and I hasten to reply Mr Reed and wife left here two weeks ago yesterday for Glen Dale they were well and in good spirits I dont anticipate they had much trouble on the road it was very pleasant all that week in fact it was the pleasantest week we have had since Ellen came from Vt it is very cold here this the snow is about two foot deep on the level it has snowed and rained alternately and then froze together so solid that they drive teames any where on the drifts without breaking in I expect Willard down again in March after the rest of his goods and a yoke of steers that he left here

Yours Respectfully
Elmira Talcott

Even after so many months had passed, Willard had no house of his own to take his wife; instead they had to stay in a room at the Lyon's for several months. Willard and Stoughton left early each morning and walked about a mile to their land, not returning until evening. Ellen had to stay there alone. Making matters worse for Ellen, the mail did not go "regular." The nearest post office was sixteen miles away in Mauston; it was so cold and the snow so deep that letters were precious and scarce. Letters took five weeks and longer, instead of the usual ten days or so, to arrive from Vermont now, and that was only if someone was kind enough to bring them all the way from Mauston. It was not until March 8th, when there was a thaw that carried off part of the snow, that the man down the road returned from Mauston and left a thick letter at Lyon's for Ellen. It was from her parents dated February 1. They were worried and scolding her that they had not heard from her. Ellen felt frustrated. It was not her fault. She had written them, and long letters too.

The pangs of loneliness were ever present in Ellen's life; yet somehow she endured the seemingly unending days, the bouts of homesickness. Then there was new hope: Leonora's sister-in-law and Ellen's dear friend, Esther, had written Ellen's mother. She and Lewis would be visiting Ellen soon in the West — if they could find her.

Esther Bagley Cline to Arterista Spaulding...

Feb. 9 1857
North Stockholmn [N.Y.]
Dear Friend
I have now seated myself for the purpose of writing to you not knowing whether you will except of it or not on account of being so long neglected but not forgot I should have writen before if Ellen had not been with you and I knew when I wrote to her it would answer for both (or at least I thought it would) as for my healths it is better for a week or so I think I have got completely over the dreadful cold I got in the fall and has laid me up the

86

most of the winter   Lewis and Edgar are well   L is
getting out shingle bolts   he get two Dollars a cord in the
woods for them   he starts in March for Wisconsin   I
intended to have staid here but am so much better he thinks
I had better when he does   I shall go and stay a week
with Ellen if I can find her   I would not miss seeing
her for nothing and I do believe she would like to see me
she has not answered my last letter for some reason   I sent
it to Ludlow not knowing that she had left   I wish you
would write as soon as you get this and tell me where to
direct a letter to her for I want her to know that we shall
see each other in a short time   she has always writen to me
to go and now if nothing hapens I shall   how glad I
am

As for the weather here it beautiful   We had an
awful storm last week and so bitter cold and then after it
had snowed and blowed like a hurricane for four day it
grew warm   commenced raining and now not a bit of snow
is to be seen and quite warm and in fact we have had a
very mild winter   my dish water is hot and I must draw
to a close for I have no one now to help me and I have
got to my Journeying dress to make   L is going to get me
a nice silk before I go   I want black and he wants light
I will send a peice when I get it   love to all   write
soon   from your sincere friend   E Cline

With relief after a long wait, Arterista and Stedman read Ellen's letter.

Glendale   March 8th 1857

Dear Father and Mother,

We have just received your letter of Feb,, 1st to night, and we was very glad to hear from you once more, and hear you was all well, we are well, and hope these lines will find you the same. you wrote you had not heard from us, it is not our fault   we have wrote you, but you know it has been very bad going every where this winter, and the mail does not go regular.[54] It has been very cold and the snow very deep, but we have had one thaw, and carried off part of the snow, so folks can just begin to get into the woods to get their fire wood. Willard thinks he can get his timber out so as to get his house up next month, but if it is up in three I wont complain. I am sory we could not have got Esthers letter sooner, for I am affraid it is to late to have them get one from us, but I have got Willard to write to them while I write this, so they will start tomorrow   I should be very glad to have them come out if they would be contented, for I am very lonely out here all alone. I wish you could let your farm and come out, but do not sell it for perhaps you would not like out here. I went a visiting three times last week. I like the folks what I have seen of them much better than I did down to Burke. I was very glad to hear Leonora was getting along so well and hope she will keep up smart this time, but I think she might have found a prettier name if she had tried.[55] I think you had a great time with your thresher. tell Mr Lamb he must leave his old cat in the back window next time and I guess there wont any body get in. I wish you would write where George is if you have heard from him, for we have not heard a word since he lift us the next Monday after we got home. I should think John has jumped out of the frying pan into the fire haint he, where is Harvey going too now live on the interest of his money I suppose. I suppose Aunt Lucy[56] is in her glory if she has got her a silk dress. It was too bad Mrs Dewy could not have had her baby donation night so they could had another present. I got a letter from Maria a few days ago, they was all well. Charles & Emilie[57] had got to keep-ing house. I want you should answer this immediately and write about all the young folks and old ones too, give our love to Grandsire and Grand ma and tell them this is the awfulest country they ever heard of. I wish they was out here. Collins done as much keeping school as I expected he would. I do not think of any thing more to write this time and it is getting bed time so I will bid you good night and close, write soon,

We send our love to you all,
Yours affectionately
Ellen E Reed

One month since she last wrote, Esther Cline again wrote to Ellen's mother in Ludlow, Vermont.

North Stockholmn
May 9 [1857]

Dear Friend

I have now a spare moment and I will scratch a few lines for you   I am pretty well draged out   We start for Wis this afternoon   hope I shall have good luck and in a short time shall [see] Ellen   Willard wrot to Lewis to go and stop with them   we shall stay a week or two   I wish you were going with but I suppose that is out of the question   I guess L will buy a place of Willard he wrote that he would sell him one if he liked   Will be so lucky as to live near Ellen in a strange land   I am as well as can be expected but I cant write any more for the time flies past   give my love to those that want and remember that where ever we go you will be remembered as a dear cherished friend   Write and direct the same as you do Ellens   I hope in a few years we shall se and yours out there   good by for the present
Esther Cline

The first of May, after months of promises, Willard finally moved Ellen into a temporary place of her own. Standing there on the prairie, the dense woods and river to its back, the shanty must have looked so humble, but after nearly six months of staying in small rooms in others' homes, Ellen probably did not complain. Her first house, the log cabin down in Burke, was a mansion next to this.

True, it was about the same size, but her new shanty only had the one room. There was no chamber upstairs, and it was much more crudely built. Now her kitchen was outdoors. It was May already; there was no need for Willard to build a hearth, and soon it was going to be too hot to have the stove inside anyway.

Willard already had their wheat and oats in the ground and some of the garden made too, for he was calculating to have a good garden this year, if it was possible with the weather and all, for Ellen's folks were coming in the fall. Maybe even Arterista's parents, Grandsire and Grandma Haven. In a few days, Willard planned to work on the house — he had calculated to be in their poplar log house nearly one year earlier. It would stand ten rods from the river there on the east side of the woods in the prairie land, but on higher ground.

Esther and Lewis were coming any day now, and Ellen had nothing to give them but biscuits and butter. Esther might not be contented living like poor folks; worse yet, she might not want to stay. Unfortunately, there was nothing Ellen could do. Provisions were scarce and prices high everywhere in the Western Country.

Ellen had become bored and lonely in her log shanty. Willard and Stoughton would go off soon after the sun came up, returning at midday for dinner, then at dusk for supper. But dinner and supper were probably the same fare anyway — biscuits, butter and tea, along with the little milk they had, divided among the three of them. Strangely, Stoughton and Willard were gaining pounds while Ellen was only growing thinner.

After dinner the men would head back into the woods. Then Ellen was unable to see them, the huge trees and thick tangled brush in her way. She would not see them again until nearly dusk. Unlike at Burke, Ellen did not have much work to do. She did not have cream to churn into butter, nor enough milk to make into cheese. She only had her washing, which she had to do outside in a tub of boiling water.

Finally one day Ellen forgot her pride of being a lady. Esther and Lewis were supposed to be coming any day, but she would not wait all alone at the shanty anymore. Instead, she was determined to go into the woods with Stoughton and Willard and help them get out rails. And that is what she did — she just rucked up her long dress and petticoats and went into the woods like the men. Of course, she would *never* tell anyone.

Over two months had passed since Ellen last wrote to her parents. She sat down inside her little log shanty, picked up a pencil, and filled her sheet of paper finishing with a note at the top of the page:

I think your dress and aprons very pretty, and Grandmas quilt I wish I could come and help her quilt it, be sure and come out all of you this Fall.

Glendale May 13th 1857

Dear Father & Mother

I am almost ashamed to write to you, for I have waited so long, but better late than not at all, the mail does not go regular and we do not have a chance to send letters as we used to down to Burke. We are all well as usual and hope these lines will find you the same. I want to know how that sore is on your ankle. Willard & Stoughton want I should tell you they are getting saucy ragged and fat every day. they are cutting rails to day. the wheat and oats are in the groung and some of the garden is made, we are calculateing to have a good garden this year if it is a possible thing for we shall expect you out this fall and Grandsire & Grand ma and we don't want to be disappointed neither. Willard has put up a little log shanty, that is 11 by 13 feet, and we have mooved up here into that, it was so far for them to come up from Mr Lyons, he is going to work on the other in a few days. I shall be glad when it is done. It has been a very cold late spring we have not had any rain but it is cold and windy to day and looks like rain. if it does not come warm soon, so things can grow I do not know what people will do, for provision is very scarce and high, my butter is not quite gone yet, but the cheese is gone, it was good and I wish I had some more. we have got two cows, one of them gives milk and the other one is expected to some time if nothing happens. we have got 16 hens so I think we shall raise some chickens this summer. you wanted to know how I liked up here, it is a very lonely place I think, not near so pleasant as it was down to Burke, but it is a better place I suppose takeing all things in consideration. there is plenty of wood and soft water. you wanted to know what the neighbors names was. they are such odd names some of them that I can hardly remember them, the nearest ones are Lile one side and Hall the other, then there is Rossman, Telfer, Neff, Fowler, Deo, and others too bad to write. Mrs. Robbins, (where Willard boarded last summer,) is dead, she died a week ago last Thursday. I like the folks up here better than I did down, there. I have had company once since we come up here. Mr

Talcot has bought a place down nine miles from Portage. We have had several letters from Esther and have been expecting them every day for some time but they do not come yet, perhaps they did not get our letter, if you know where they are I wish you would write to them that we are expecting them and hope they will come. write us as soon as you get this, and write about every body and every thing. I do not think of any thing more this time, so goodby We all send our love to all, and respects to every body. Ivory has not been here yet.

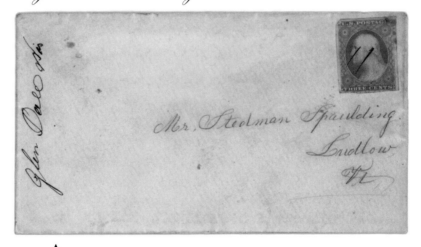

At long last, Esther, Lewis, and young Edgar found Ellen and Willard's humble abode in Glendale. (They left New England May 9th and arrived shortly after Ellen's letter of the 13th.) Esther had listened to her husband talk of their great opportunity and the fertile land so much that she actually had held high expectations herself. But she was not one to let her pride hide the facts; finally someone was there to tell those back home the truth about the West. In her letter to Arterista and Stedman, Esther also told what Ellen *really* was doing out there to keep from being lonely.

Glendale June 6 [1857]

Dear Friend,

After so long a time I have retired to my room
(Would that you could see it) for the purpose of giving you
a short sketch of Western life   When we arrived at Glendale after along tedious journey I must say I was sadly
disapointed but a short distance from that great and
flourishing viliage which contains one store and two
dwelling huts we found where Ellen lived and she was just
coming out of the woods with the men she had been
splitting rails with them but she and Willard appeared glad
to see us and soon got us supper and as it was night we
soon went to bed but I was to tired and homesick to sleep
and had I belonged to the flying family daylight would
found me in york state where the frost kills the corn in
August but morning came and I ventured to look out door
again but every thing looked dreary to me but Lewis was
perfectly satisfied so I thought perhaps it was a good place
and I would try to make the best of it till I knew and
see more but who wouldent have been homesick   I was
tired and Edgar was ugly as a little snipe and then must
have the mump and then the scarlet fever but he has got
over them now and acts like a rational being and I have
got rested and things look very different to me   I find
myself in one of the most delightful counties in Wisconsin
and in a few years the part we live in will look very

95

different from from what it does now for there is a great chance for building up a great place on acount of the water priviledge and the great distance from all kinds of mills It does not take a sensible person long to learn the first lesson after he gets here and when he has learnt that he is ready to commence work perhaps you would like to know what this important lesson is I can tell you but you cannot realize it till you get here it is this that living and getting rich in a new country is not the work of a day nor a year but people are obliged scratch for a while for every thing is to be done and done at great disadvantage but time and perseverance will make us wealthy and happy and as our husbands will lead us abroad over their well cultivates farms and at evening sit down and laugh over days gone by we shall be well paid for all Would that some of the eastern ladies that are dying for the want of air or going in to fits at the sight of a bug or worm was here I for one would be happy to give them a place in my log mansion as soon as it is finished true it is not very agreable to see adders or rattle snakes crawling through the crack or go to bed at night thinking we must have them for a bedfellow before morning but after all these cracks are very useful for when the wind blowes in at the door when we sweep we can poke the dirt down the cracks out of sight and keep it clean around the outside of the door but give me a home here for all any where else for though I have been here but a short time I feel well paid for all I sufferd in getting here   our crops look very nice and farmers have every thing to encourage them even amid their hardships and who is there that stand and look abrod over the beautiful prairies or travel over them and behold the flours more numerous and beautiful than can be cultivated in eastern gardens and then say this is home for me   true there is some from the east that have left friend behind nearer and dearer to them than any thing Wisconsin affords   such of cours see many sad and heart aching hours   I wish such ones could have their friends with for it seem hard to see them unhappy in a land like this when the presence of friends is all that is needed to make them happy   I hope you ar making calculations to come out here this fall for we all want to see you very much and would run with out streched arms to meet you and if you only knew how anxious Ellen is to have you come you would arrange affairs so as to be here this fall   I asked her to write in this as there is room but she said she could not and wantes I should tell you when she felt as though she could writ she would but she wanted to say so much she did not know whore to begin   she wants to know if you are coming out here this fall or next spring or if you intend to have her spend her days here alone   I wish for her sake you could come and I think it would be for Willard's interest to have Mr Spaulding here a year I do not know of anything more to write   Write to me

and let me know all the news that for me to know and
I want to know all about your ancle   What ails it and
if it is anything dangerous   I have thought a great deal
about it   I shall now close by telling you that we are
all comfortabl well and send our love to all inquiring friends
this from your friend
Mrs Esther Cline
now write soon for it takes so long to get a letter

Finally, two months after her last letter to her parents, Ellen got
out her pen, ink, and a small folded sheet of paper.

Tell George we wish he would appear to us as he did once
before, but if not to fat the rooster for thanks giving and
invite us to supper.   I should think Grandsire could live
some where else and let you come out here.
We send our love to every body, write often   I went a
visiting the other day, dont you want to know what we
had for supper   it was boiled potatoes and thickned gravy
and dry wheat bread without any butter, and it was good
enough for the king
Glendale, July 18 th [1857]
Dear Father & Mother,
As it is a long time since I have wrote you
I thought I would try and write this morning, and
thought perhaps you would like to hear from your children
in the woods.   The folks are all well, my health is good

98

excepting a bad cough but that is nothing. I should like to know how your ankle is and what ails it and what you think about it. It is very healthy about here this summer, we have had fine weather, the crops looks first rate, it was the hotest day yestoday I ever saw I should think, but we had a shower last night and it is a little cooler to day. we have not had any strawberrys but are going to have blueberrys. Willard and Co. have got six acres broke on their place and nine or ten down on mine I have got the best place in town. they are going to haying next week and then after that I expect the house will be put up. I wish you could see what a nice house I have got, the stove is out doors so my kitchen is as big as any body has got. I wish you would come out here and stay one year so you could see how folks live out West to get rich. there is one family in the neighborhood that had nothing for three or four meels but thick sour milk, and others live on nothing but boiled wheat, and some on indian meal, alone and some on flour, now I suppose you will say that is all shiflessness, and it is some, but you have no idea, the place is new and every thing scarce and high, it is sixteen miles to a store or tavern and twenty to mill, and it is not very convenient going every day. you need not think we are starving for we are not, no, we are living out West getting rich thats the talk, so never mind, but it wont always be so, you know very well who encouraged Willard, and who has been out here to see him.

he says you neither come to see him, nor write for him to come, but still supposes you would like to see him. it has been hard times every where this summer. money is very scarce, it is from 12 to 50 per cent. Lewis folks are well, his Father Mother brother and sister come with them and are expecting a sister and two brothers more this fall. Esther thinks it rather poor living on biscuits and butter, without potatoes or meat but there is none in the country to be bought. it will do them good. I wish there was more of the big bugs that have always lived on honney, had to come down to that, (I guess she will want to get to Leonoras butry [58] as bad as she did last summer) but there is better times comeing   Lewis has not got his things. I want you should write as soon as you get this, and write the particulars abut your ankle, and every thing you can think of. Tell Grand ma I have not had one ride on my saddle yet aint it to bad, poor folks have to do as they can, while rich ones do as they are a mind to. we had a letter from Maria a few days ago   they was well. they want Willard to go and buy the Upham place there. Stoughton is as hearty as a bear and almost as black, but he is a good boy, yes, one of the best. he got a letter from Ivory a few days a go, he was well. my sheet is full so I must stop, but if I could see you I could tell you things that would make you stare. this is a piece of my apron.

I have killed one rattle snake

Ellen placed a piece of cloth from the new dress she was making inside the folded sheet of paper. Then she folded the paper over three times so that it would fit into the small envelope. Ellen knew that this would be a special piece of cloth from the Western Country. Soon it probably would be cut and pieced into a block for her mother's or grandmother's new quilt.

Since the beginning of May, Ellen, Willard, and Stoughton were living in the crude, tiny "shanty," as Ellen called it. When Esther, Lewis, and their child Edgar arrived, all six of them lived in the one room. Before, Ellen had complained of being lonely. Now she had three more and one of them little, sick, crying, and whining. She had no privacy. It was damp and hot inside the shanty. With the door propped open, however, every tiny flying thing came in to cause them more misery.

But there were those who did not even have a shanty. People were living "so poor" all around. Lewis had brought his folks along with his younger brother and sister and was expecting two more brothers in the fall. With times so hard, Ellen had all she could do to feed Lewis, Esther, and Edgar, let alone so many more.

Their faces drawn in lines of worry, the men talked in alarmed voices of the troubled times. The Panic of 1857, as it would be called in the future, had devastating effects on the Western Country. It was more to haul freight from Milwaukee to Madison than from the eastern ports to Madison. It wasn't right. It cost as much as hauling by wagon to Milwaukee. There just was no way for a farmer to make out on his wheat. The railroad's rate was so high because there was no other line. It was cheaper for Iowa and Minnesota farmers to get their wheat to Milwaukee than for Glendale farmers. Some farmers were thinking it was cheaper to burn their corn or wheat for fuel than to try to get it to market. But there were hard times everywhere. And the times were only to get worse. The banks and corporations were crashing all over the east, railroads going bankrupt, land value dropping overnight. Money was so scarce, and they couldn't "get trusted to the stores" anymore.

In spite of the hard times, Willard was working all the time now on the log house. He was building it out of poplar so it would be an attractive, light-colored cabin, the interior not as dark and gloomy as an oak or pine one. And it would have two floors so they would have more room. It was September already, and Willard was determined they should get into their new house before cold set in. Finally Willard and Lewis split all the shingles, nailed them down in a day, chinked the interstices between the logs, and then laid loose boards for the upper floor. Only the structural part of the house was completed. There was no floor, only the dirt of the prairie. The house was stark and cold inside, but Willard was determined — they were moving in nonetheless. It was October already; Willard could go about finishing it while they were inside. He'd just lay down some loose boards across the floor joists upstairs so that Ellen could stay up there while he put in the partitions and flooring down below.

Ellen did not feel as well as she had. She was coughing more and more and found herself able to do less. All the pounding and banging downstairs, along with the sawdust and dirt, probably added to her illness. Willard talked of going south for her health, but there was only one direction Ellen yearned to go, sick or well. The Upham place was even for sale in Willard's hometown of Chelmsford, Massachusetts. Willard's folks thought he should buy it, but he would not hear of it. He still thought he would get rich in the West. But it was already three years since they had come to Wisconsin, and they appeared to be poorer than the day they had arrived.

Three months since Willard last wrote to Vermont...

Glendale Oct 12th „57

Dear Father & Mother

I write to let you know that we are well as usual with the exception of Ellens, cough and that is some better. she is taking Wistars Balsam of Wild Cherry[59] I think it would be beneficial to her, to go South this winter, to a warmer climate, and I think we should if we had any friends or acquaintances to go to. there are two of my old school mates at Rock Island Illinois, but that is not far enough South to make much difference with the climate. I should like to see you out here this fall, but I have given up the idea of your coming at all. still it seems as if you could leave home If you was to try hard, „ where there is a will there is a way „   well I am not going to tell you that we are coming home this winter, because we do not intend to come if we can get you out here. we have delayed writing week after week for a long time waiting to hear from you, but no letters come. we are spliting rails now for a cowyard. we have got to start the plow soon, for it does better to fall plow for wheat and oats, and it saves time in the Spring. it will take us two or three weeks, and then we are into the woods again. I wish you would soon as you get this write and let us know what the calculation is about coming out, so that we shall know what to depend upon, but my sheet is full and I must close.

I remain yours
JW Reed

Two weeks later, Ellen found an unusually large sheet of faintly lined, ivory paper and wrote an alarming letter to her parents. No longer did she hide the real truth because of her pride. Her daily existence was too serious, far too grim to cover over with pride.

Stoughton got a letter from Ivory yesterday, he was well we send our love to all our friends and acquaintences

Glen Dale Oct 25 th 1857

Dear Father & Mother,

We received your long looked for letter yesterday, and was very glad to hear from you once more. we have wrote two or three letters, and received no answer, and did not know but you had forgot where we were. We was glad to hear you was all so well, but sory to hear of your having such hard times and bad luck with your potatoes. I hope you will never see any harder times than now, but if you dont, (unless it is worse than I can learn) I cannot think you will ever know what hard times are, although it may seem hard to you. You wanted to know if we expected you out in the spring. I suppose you remember what the calculation was, and what you promised me the last thing last fall, if so what can you expect. We have expected you next spring, but if you do not want to see us, you need not come, and I see from what you wrote that you think it an awful job, little did I think three long years ago, that my own Father &

Mother would not have come to see me for so long, and then thought it a hadship, imagine yourself in just such a spot as I am, fifteen hundred miles from home, and every thing, that is near and dear to you, as I am, (except one of the kindest and best husbands that God ever let live,) and you wont feell much different from what I do. My health has been very poor ever since I came out here last fall, and I do not think it is much better nor looks very incourageing for me. I have a very hard cough all of the time, and have had hard colds one after the other all summer and fall, I am takeing Wisters Balsom of wild Cherry and think it helps me some, and would a great deel more if I had half a chance for my life, but you think it is hard times there where you have enough of every thing, but I guess if you was out here as we, and thousands of others have been, you would not call that hard, but we have been obliged to live so because we could not get our money for things that we sold nor where it was due us. Lewis paid three hundred and that was all, and that had to go for big debts and for oxen which we must have to work the land with, and then he was out and could not get their things nor has not got them yet, and we had to divide the last mouthfull of provission with them and we have lived short, yes what you would call short, but we think we are well off, and hope never to be any worse. he is expecting his brother from the east soon and then I hope he will pay us, but money is very scarce out

105

here, and all kinds of grain is down low and every thing we have to buy is very high and we can not get trusted to the stores any, (I am glad of that), so we can live without. Willard has been barefoot or just as bad all the fall, because they had no boots at Mauston till the other day he made out to borrow a pair to wear out and went afoot 16 miles to get a pair, so now he is not barefooted any more. We have had two cows this summer one was a farrow one and gives milk and the other one was fatted and killed, so we had meat a while but we had to sell the most of her for the neighbors was crying around the door for beef, but we have not had any meat lately, nor a speck of butter for weeks and weeks, there is none in the country to be bought, so there it is again, and we cant get a cow till we get some money so we live on potatoe and salt with a little milk on it, and bread without butter, and have lived weeks this summer without a speck of sugar in the house, and have three or four ladies some out from Mauston, and nothing for tea but biscuit and a little butter I had some then and tea, but that is nothing it is out wist in the land that flows with milk and honey. We are living in our new house made of Popple logs, it is not done yet but I can live up stairs (only it is a ladder) on a rough loose floor, waiting for them to get the lower floor done it is part done, they are to work for Lewis shingleing his house to day, it had to be done for they could not stay where they are another day it is Sunday but that cannot be helped, they have had to work sundays or not at all for it has rained half of the time this summer. Stoughton thought the other day if he had forty hands and as many more feet he could get something done, he is well and is steady and does first rate, and thinks this high living but that is nothing when he can step to the window and look out on his great farm, and it is some so with me when I look at the land and then at the notes on twelve percent to the amount of from one to two thousand dollar, (yes I wont pleed poverty for I have always heard enough of that) and then sit down to potato and salt it goes first rate and I wonder what poor folks do that have not got any potatoes. Willard & Stoughton are going to dig their potatoes (which have rotted some), this week and then are going to plowing and getting out rails. We have talked some of coeming home this winter, but I do not know as we shall. Willard thinks it will be better for me and him too, to go down south and I do not know where we shall go, but if we can get money we shall go somewhere. he says if you cant find any one else to take your place next year so you can come out, he will go and carry it on. that piece I sent you in his letter was a piece of my new dress. I have got my knitting and sewing most done. I have done my work with what Willard helps me, all but my washing. I have not washed a thing but twice since early last spring, and you need not think it is the seven nor nine month consumption that ails me either, if you do you are mistaken.

I do not think of any thing more this time and my sheet is full so I will close, write soon

(Ellen had so much to say that she covered the four sides of her sheet running out of room for her name on the back. Instead she wrapped her closing around to the very bottom of the first page.)

as you get this, Ellen E Reed

One month later, on November 30, 1857, Lewis Cline's sister, Lucy, moved into Ellen and Willard's log house as house-keeper, maid, companion, and (probably unspoken yet necessary) as Ellen's nurse. Whether Willard's or Ellen's idea to hire Lucy, the reality was that Ellen could no longer keep house herself. Here was this eighteen-year-old, the picture of health, moving about in Ellen's house quickly, energetically, shaking and turning the ticks, tightening the rope bed, sweeping the floor, washing and drying the dishes, mixing up biscuits, carrying in firewood. She moved about with strength, moving things easily in her way, never complaining. She did the things a good wife should do. Lucy's presence was a constant reminder to Ellen of her failing health: somewhere within her consciousness Ellen had to admit to herself the doctor's terrifying diagnosis — the "seven or nine month consumption."

Nearly three months since her last letter, Ellen wrote to her parents...

Glen dale, Jan 19th, 1858.

Dear Father, & Mother,
I will now try and answer your kind letter of last year which was gladly received, and we was glad to hear you were all well, and enjoying yourselves so

well, and hope these lines will find you the same. We are
well as usual here. I am takeing medicin all the time but
I do not see as it does me much good, my cough is not quite
as bad as it was last summer but it is bad enough yet, but I
think my livver is worse than my lungs. I have an awful
time every few weeks with my stomach, which is caused by
my livver,s sweling. Lowises sister Lucy is working for me
she came here the last day of Nov, and I guess I shall
keep her till you come, for I am so lonely here all alone that
I can not stan it. We have got a few neighbors but they are
all tied at home with babies. I wont say any more about
them, you will see when you get here. I want you should
come as soon as you can, it seems a long time to wait, the rail
road is done so you can come to Milwaukee and then to
Mauston where Willard will meet you with a nice span of
horned horses and a Wisconsin buggy if you will tell us
when you will be there. I want you should bring my
shoulder brases. I want to know where the western folks are,
that would not live out here and went back, them are the
kind they had independents enough to go back and let folks
know they did not like out here

Willard and Stoughton are getting out rails they
have got to get and lay up in fence four thousand between
this and puting in crop time in the spring. It has been quite
warm the most of the time, we have had about six inches of
snow. Stoughton has been down to see Ivory he was well.

Willard has been down to Burke. he found the folks all well, but Mrs Harris she was not expected to live long.[60] *Willard bought me a pony, and I have rode her twice, but it is too cold for me to ride this winter I suppose you have been expecting us there, but you will be disappointed as well as we. we was disappointed in getting as much money as we expected, when I wrote before, of some of the rich folks that are oweing us. I should like to know where George is we have not heard from him for a long time, and I should like to know where and what Miriam Keyes is, and all the rest of the young folks. I will send you a piece of another new dress Willard got me down to Burke*[61] *I do not think of anything more to write this time so I will bid you good by once more, and close,*

we all send our love to you all. tell Grandsir and Grand ma we want them to come with you, how I wish I could see them

Write soon

Yours truly
E E Reed

The grim news about Lucy Ann Spaulding Harris, George's oldest girl, may have struck too close to home. Only twenty-four years of age with little ones that needed her, Lucy Ann had consumption and was not expected to live long.

The disease was everywhere, and no one knew how someone got it. It was the strangest thing — one of the family coughing and wasting away while brothers and sisters, mother and father,

Emily Emerson Reed, Ellen's sister-in-law.
Photograph courtesy of George Adams Parkhurst.

husband and children all looked on healthy, "smart as lightning," and totally unable to help.

One month since his last letter, Willard wrote the final details and instructions for Arterista and Stedman prior to their departure for Wisconsin, but first Ellen penciled a note:

Glen Dale   Feb 21ˢᵗ 1858
Lucy Cline would like to have you get her a brown hat like Emilys[62] if you can without too much trouble, not over one dollar and a quarter

Dear Father & Mother

　　　I write a few lines to let you know that yours of the 11th of Jan was gladly received. we sent you a letter a short time before, and have been waiting for an answer, but thought we would not wait long. Stoughton & I are tough and hearty as bears, Ellen,s health is about the same, I think her cough is not quite so bad as it has been at times. we are looking forward to the time when we shall see you here, which I suppose will be in about a month. I think you had better not bring any thing but what clothes you will need here. I do not think of any thing to send to you for except a few pounds of tea, for we do not get much here that is good. we have had a very mild winter there was not a cold day in December or January but this month we have had now and then a cold day, with and snow enough for decent sleding we are geting out rails now we have hauled over two thousand, and have got fifteen hundred more to get we intend to fence in three fortys this winter. when you come out come to Mauston by way of Millwaukee. there stop at the Parish House, inquire for the Fowler Settlement. it is fourteen miles from Fowlers to Mauston, and we live two miles from Fowlers If I could know what day you would be at Mauston I would be there to meet you, if not you can get a livery team to take you out here   as

I do not think of any thing more I will close. write soon as you get this.

I remain yours
J. W. Reed

On Sunday, April 11, 1858, Stedman and Arterista Spaulding finally arrived at Ellen and Willard's poplar, log house, two miles down the narrow, rutted road from the Fowler Settlement. Stedman had paid five dollars for the livery team to travel only sixteen miles from Mauston to Glendale, more than the cost of one of their train tickets from Chicago to Milwaukee.[63]

They had journeyed fifteen hundred miles to Glendale hoping to have a wonderful visit with their daughter and son-in-law. Immediately upon their first glance of Ellen, however, the stark reality of the situation must have overcome them. From correspondence, they had no idea that indeed Ellen was dying. Instead, as Stedman later wrote, they had been hoping she would be "well and smart." They had not been prepared for the many "gloomy hours & hart rending senes that we have had to pass through."[64] There was little that Stedman, Arterista, and Willard could do now but try to make Ellen as comfortable as possible in her last weeks.

Seeing for himself that Ellen and Willard had so little food, Stedman sent Willard off to Lisbon and to Wonewoc on several occasions with money for one hundred pounds of flour, four pounds of saleratus, molasses, sugar, and "other things," as well as "Paper Leter Stamps" and money for Willard to have his plow fixed.[65] During their stay there, they ate well for the Western Country. Maybe if Ellen had been better, she would have said the biscuits and molasses were "good enough for the king." But now Stedman could only feel sorry for all the meals at his own table and his full buttery and well-stocked pantry in Vermont. Those three years Ellen had been gone, there never had been a day he had not had enough lamb, or beef, or pork, or chicken; potatoes and gravy; or cod-fish cakes swimming in molasses on Saturday nights. Now he had the money with him — money enough to fill many pantries, money enough to buy a whole hog or side of beef in New England; yet in Glendale, Wisconsin, there was none to be bought. Stedman had to suffer his own gluttony of those past years denying his daughter the money for which she begged, thinking she was spoiled and should make do on what her husband could provide her. Now Stedman would gladly give her all those things, and now he could not.

There were no more letters to Vermont until July 15, 1858. On that morning Stedman Spaulding dipped his pen into ink and forced himself to begin the saddest letter a father ever had to write.

GlenDale, Thursday Morning

Thomas & Leonora
Again I take my pen in hand to write a few lines to you, as it has been some considerable length of time since I wrote to you before. I presume you have been anxiously waiting to hear from here again but I have not forgotten you amidst the gloomy hours & hart rending senes that we have had to pass through   since then I have had many anxious thoughts about our children and Grand children in Vermont, and think the time will soon come when we shall see them again. But the News which

"I think of what I have seen of poor people I have never seen people live so poor & fair so hard as some do here... if any one does not believe me I would just say to them come and see."   Stedman Spaulding

I must tell you although shocking it may be to you all there, it is not less so to us here. But if you have seen the letter I last wrote to Grandsir Haven I suppose you cant expect any thing different from what I am a bout to write. Ellen had sustained the idea that her disorder was not the consumption and that she should get better by and by and be able to return to Vermont with us next fall or winter which She ever expressed considerable anxiety for doing and when her flesh and strength was so gone that she could not set in her chair nor bear her weight on her feet she thought still that she would start to go home if we would go with her, but the Doctor said her lungs were so much decayed that the moment we went to mooving her they would break down and she would certainly die. for a bout three weeks she had not been able to speak louder than a whisper. she had had a sorethroat and mouth except that, she complained but little of any paine at all. But the consumption was settled on her lung and she was slowly and gradually wasteing away untill at length feable nature gave way and she breathed out her last gust, Monday Eight Oclock in the after noon. Willard went to Mauston in the Morning to see the Doctor for her and get her some more Medison and returned one hour before she died. there had been no sensable alteration in her for some time and we thought it might be that she would remain so for some time. But about two hours after Willard left her she had a hard spell of coughing and raised an uncommon quantity of matter. we supposed some thing broke or gave way in her stomach at that time for she did not appear as well after that. I stayed to help take care of her and mooved her from one bed to the other as we used to do several times in the day untill noon then I went out to help Stoton lay some rail fence & in little while they sent for me to come to the house and I found she was failing verry fast she said she should not live to ever see Willard again but she did he returned just in time for her to see him and speak to him once more. she appeared to have her senses untill her last moments, and died without a struggle or a groan Alass, how panefull it is to tell you that _Ellen_ _is_ _Dead_ but so it is and soon we must all die and how important it is that we are prepaired for that great change which we must all meet. The Funeral services were attended on Wednesday afternoon Eld. Moor [66] and Eld. Harris the two Glen Dale Ministers attended. the day was verry cool & cloud, and it certainly appeared a verry solumn day to me. a collection of most of the People in this part of the Town & the goining part of Plymouth. the Neighbours all have been extremely kind to Ellen dureing her sickness & gave her all the assistance they could, for which I requested Eld. Moore to to express to them our most hearty thanks.

The grave that contains her remains is beneath the little Oaks but a few rods from the house and in plain sight of the window where I am writing, hallowed spot, the cool breeze is gently waveing the branches of the weeping Oaks over it. we intend when it comes cold weather to take her remains back to Ludlow it was her request. I think we shall stay here and keep house a spell for Willard and Stoughton unless some thing should happen to call us back.

We are enjoying verry good health here and I though if Ellen had been well and smart as we were hopeing she would be we should have taken much comfort with the folks here in this new country although they are labouring under many disadvantages which are commonly found in a place like this yet they have many thing to incourage and animate them the price of their land is

117

riseing every year   their roads are becoming better   they are breakeing and enlargeing their fields   the marshes are covered with the tall waveing grass and the riseing land a good share of it is covered with the beautifull fields of wheat and corn, and finally the whole face of the earth is dressed in its most beautifull green.

The weather ever since we come here has been verry cold dull and cloudy, except about one week of the last part of June I think was the warmest days that I ever saw any where. it commenced raining here the 27 day of may and rained every day for 14 days except one which caused the farmers to be verry late about their springs work for when it rained they could not work and when it did not rain their land was so muddy and sticky that they could do nothing with it and before it dried off it would rain again

Your letter of June 22d. we received July 3d. also one that Uncle Rylands Folks sent the same time   Ellen was so then that she could look them over and read them we were verry glad to hear that you were all so well. and as for Austin tell him Grandsir is verry sorry he has cut his foot so bad and I hope it has got well by this time so that he can go to school again.

We are all goeing to work on the road to day and I have not time to write any more now and I am ex- pecting a chance to send this out to Lisbon to day to the *post office so I must close hopeing those lines may find you and all our Friends well and comfortable and happy*

Yours Respectfully

July the 15 th 1858   *Stedman Spaulding*

(At the end of the letter was a note from Arterista.)

I will send you a lock of Ellens hare to look at   that is all I can send you now, it was cut from her head just before she was put into her coffin, Esther is some better   she was so she come to se Ellen breath her last, I want you should send this to Ludlow or carry it as soon as you can conveniently for we have not wrote to Ludlow now, we shall write to Ludlow before long, we all send our best respectes to you all, and every bod that takes pains to in-quire after us,

I must close good by, Arterista Spaulding

write soon as you get this and let us know how you all do

Until the very last, Ellen denied she was dying, pleading with her parents to take her home to Vermont. No doubt the most "hart rending" time in Stedman's entire life was having to say "No" to the one last thing his daughter wanted most in life. As much as he hated to acknowledge the doctor's diagnosis and prognosis, Stedman knew the doctor was right in not allowing her to travel.

Later, after Stedman had firmly said "No," Ellen asked again. She could only whisper; yet again she asked them to take her home to Vermont. That moment of comprehending what Ellen really meant was more than a parent should have to bear. This time Stedman gave his promise. Ellen could finally rest. She was going to go home at last.

They promised Ellen that they would take her home with them. She had been so fearful of being buried in Wisconsin soil. There had been no way to tell her the cruel truth — they could not explain such harsh, cold reality to her. It was the middle of the summer. How could they tell her that they would have to wait until it was cold, actually freezing with no chance of a warm spell, in order to take her body back? How could a father say *that* to his precious daughter? How could he tell her that it would be months, probably November or even December, till they could *consider* making the trip home with her coffin? Till then they would have to bide their time and wait....

One entire month had passed since his daughter's death. Stedman wrote another letter to his daughter and son-in-law in Vermont.

Glen Dale Sunday 3 O'Clock

Dear Thomas & Leonora
This has been one of the pleasantest days I have ever seen in Wisconsin, allmost equal to those gone by days I have seen in Vermont Stoughten is gone to meeting. Willard & I have been blackberrying and your Mother doing the work in the house. All in comfortable health I was intending to have gone up to the 4 o clock meeting this after noon but just as I was getting ready Mr.

Neff brought us in your letter & news paper of July 25 th, also a letter for Willard from his sister Maria Reed. We were verry glad to hear from you again and to hear that you all so well and smart. I should like to see My little grand children all of them again. if we all live the time will soon wear wear away and I shall meet them once more

Tell Buby Grandsir thinks he had better not have the mumps till after school is done. I should like to have him and Austin learn to write so that they can write us a few lines in the next letter that comes. Tell them and Oella that poor aunt Ellin will never come back to talk and play with them any more as she used to when she was there, when she bid them good by and left them it was for the last time she would ever see them again. I hope they will all of them remember her so that she will not be forgotten by them. She used to talk about them and wanted verry much to see them again

I am sorry to hear that aunt Sally is so slim & feeble [67] I want verry much to see her I am a fraid she will go in the same way that Ellin did I wonder why they do not write to us I wrote to them last spring I dont know whuther they got the letter. If you heard them speak about it I wish you would let me know next time you write. it is growing dark and there is about 25 Oxen

121

& Cows comeing & I should think by the tinkling that they have every one got a bell on, such musick we dont have in Vermont

Wednesday. I am keeping house alone this afternoon. Stoughton is gone down to the other place to finish cradleing oats & Willard is gone up to Col. Lyon's with the Oxen & wagon to help him stack grain and your Mother has gone up with him   it is about one mile on the road to the Village. We are haveing verry nice weather now for harvisting and Folks are verry busy now stacking their grain   we finished ours here at home this fore noon. to-morrow we are goeing down to stacking the grain on the other place which is about 1 1/2 miles down the river in the town of Plymouth & on the north side of the Baraboo here is a meadow from about a mile above here all the way down for three miles below here some thing like that from Ludlow to Cavendish, the the land I think is much richer than that is   some of it is coverd with trees logs & brush   some of it has been mowed and bears grass weeds & prairia flowers 2 or 3 tons to the acre. I think when it is cleared up & fixed suitable for mowing it will bear a bundance of good quality of hay. We have not began hayeing here yet but think we shall begin in a few days probably not near all the hay on the meadow will be cut it never has been. hay here last spring was worth only two dollars a ton, there is fifty tons on the meadow now that was cut last year, the plowed land is on the swells back each way from the River and has to be fenc'd in   these swells are all cut ut by ravenes that afford pastureing for the cattle and then the cattle go back over the Ridges and bluffs as far as they have a mind to go & sometimes they get so far away we dont find the cows at night. these Ridges & swells are covered with Oaks principally except some openings where the fire has burnt so hard as to burn the timber and kill it all off. I have seen places of an hundred acres that had not a green tree on it, growing up with brush again. the woods here are ful of brush of every kind.   we cant go through them with out tearing our cloths all off of us, and some times treading on a rattle Sneak

We have not been about much to see the country since we came here except to Burk   we started the next week after Ellen died and went out to Mauston sixteen miles with Mr. Fouler's team that was goeing out & stayed over night there   the next morning at 4 O.Clock we took the cars to Portage City, thirty six miles   then we got on the stag & went to Burk thirty to George and Nathan Spauldings and stayed till saturday   then George took his horses & carriage and his Wife and went down to Union with us thirty miles further to Albert Adams, had a verry good visit with them   went to meeting sunday & saw Mr. Pettegrew and his family there and a good many other

Ludlow folks   we found them all well & doing firs rate
I went to see Mr. Sawtell   he has got a nice farm & is
farming ont Vermont style   he had all his last years grain
on hand & will double on the price on it in keeping it over.
we come back to Burk Monday   stoped at Madison
Citty to see Mrs. Conly George's daughter, and returned
to Mauston friday night   stayed till the next morning
when Willard come out after us and carried us back to Glen
Dale. it is a verry good looking country down that way,
there is an immence sight of grain sowed down there   the
wheat fields cover the ground as far as I can see. One man
there has twelve hundred acres of grain on his farm but the
growth this year is uncommonly small George Spaulding
said their crops this year all look as if the land was exausted
I saw a great manny four horse reapers cutting down their
15 to 20 acres in a day but a great deal of it was not worth
more than enough to pay the expence of harvisting not only
a small growth of wheat but it is so badly blasted that it is
all most worthless, it rained so much last spring & the ground
was so wet that it was late before the crops could be put in
that they have done miserably in the whole of the western
country. the corn is verry late & backward   unless we have
a verry warm fall to ripen it off we sh[all] not get much
corn this year   I am afraid the Peopl here are a going to
be worse off this year than they were last for last year grain

124

was so plenty & money so scarce they could not sell a bushel of grain for money at any price and this year they will not raise enough to live on. here is fammilies in this town that have been liveing verry poor all summer some with out milk and some with out meat liveing on faith and hope, all most entirely naked for clothes thinking they should raise some thing this year and now their crops are all most an entire failure. I think of what I have seen of poor people I have never seen people live so poor & fair so hard as some do here, but I will write no more about that now if any one does not believe me I would just say to them come and see.

It is geting to be night the sun is sinking behind the western hill the tinkling cowbells begin to come around we have about twenty head of cattle to lay in the road opposite the house every night

and I must again bid you all good by hopeing these few lines may find you in good health and enjoying the comforts of life with cheerfulnes I hope you will write often as you can

August the 18 th, 1858   Stedman Spaulding

Thursday morning all well, verry cold but no frost yet the meadow is covered with fog. is there going to be plenty of apples this fall I am now goeing down to Fowlers post office to carry some letters 3 miles [68]

The long days lengthened to yet longer ones as the sun beat down onto his daughter's grave, the rains etching out miniature river beds into the earth, the loosed earth settling, sinking ponderously onto the crude wooden coffin, tender blades of grass sprouting up through the packed, pitiless earth.

It was not finished — he should yet have to tear away all that ground and reclaim his daughter. If only the heat would cease from the land, if only winter would come quickly this year....

And as Stedman and Arterista waited, a very sad letter came addressed to them: Arterista's mother, Lydia Haven, the real quilter of the family, had died only six weeks after Ellen. [69]

It was not until December, five months after Ellen's death, that Stedman and Arterista could finally begin their journey home. Stedman and Arterista had been in Wisconsin eight months during the hardest times the Western Country had ever known. They had been there long enough to identify with the plight of those having to "live so poor." Their experiences of those past months would be a part of them for as long as they would live. Those folks in Wisconsin were their friends, some of them almost like family; their suffering and hardships a personal burden to them, too, now. But what would have been most important to Ellen, after living there himself Stedman could understand his daughter and the words of her letters. He respected her. He was proud of her — she had struggled and sought to survive. His daughter, who could have had the best in New England, had done the best she could in such a poor existence. "I have never seen people live so poor & fair so hard as some do here...if any one does not believe me I would say to them come and see," [70] wrote Stedman in defense of his daughter.

In December in the *New York Tribune*, Horace Greeley officially reported to the world that which Ellen and Stedman had experienced firsthand. "The West is very poor," he wrote from

Racine, Wisconsin. "I think a larger proportion of the people of Michigan, Indiana, Illinois, Wisconsin, and Iowa are under the harrow now than at any former period. There is no real lack of money, provided one has wherewith to buy it; and what passes for money is a better article than that which usurped the name a year ago; but real estate, mortgages, railroad stocks and bonds, notes of hand, and promises of all kinds are not the sort of property that easily tempts a moneyed man to open his safe or his pocket-book. There is on all hands such a super-abundance of debt of various kinds that promises are a drug, and faith in human solvency sadly alloyed by scepticism. Very many want to borrow; very few are anxious to lend, no matter at what rate or on what security. Railroads partly constructed, and there stopped for want of means; blocks of buildings ditto; counties and cities involved by the issue of railroad bonds, and practically insolvent; individuals striving to stave off the satisfaction of debts, obligations, judgments, executions — such is the all but universal condition." Increasing the gravity of the situation, Horace Greeley added that the farmer's crops of 1858 were poor. [71]

Stedman took out his small ledger from his pocket, and opening it to an empty page, recorded the expenses paid out so far. "Excess baggage" — that was what they called the handmade wooden box with his daughter's remains at the depot in Mauston. $11.63 to Milwaukee and $1.25 to move it from depot to depot. [72] The scarred wooden box was slid onto the floor of the cars, shoved to the back, and stacked with baggage and produce. It was a grim journey, but they had known all along — ever since Ellen had asked — that it would be a very long, sad trip.

Chicago, From Depot to Depot .75 Supper .50
Ex Bagage to Buffalo Toledo 4.00 Breakfast 1.00

Stedman continued to pencil into his ledger. In Toledo, he wired a "telegraph" to Ludlow of their expected arrival. He would see his children soon. Otherwise, he continued the ledger as the miles passed under him:

Supper Cleveland 1.00 Ex Bagage Buffalo 3.20 Supper Syracuse .75 Albany Exchange 1.50 Conveying Bagage to & from 1.13 Express Bill to Rutland 1.00 Express Bill to Ludlow .75 Tickets to Ludlow 1.50 From Depot Ludlow .30 .[73]

They had hurried home the first chance they could; yet they arrived too late in Vermont. The ground was frozen. There was no way to get a shovel through it anymore that winter. Ellen's body would have to wait in storage until spring.

Three months after Stedman and Arterista returned to Ludlow with their daughter's remains, George Spaulding wrote a letter from Token Creek. He, too, had lost a daughter to consumption. Lucy Ann had died on March 15, four months before Ellen. At the end of his letter he added,

Mrs Spaulding says she has thot of you ever so much about carreing your child back with you as she was in stead of her being in health   the sorrows we feel for the loss of our children makes the path of life gloomy and dark to us all. [74]

Roses chiseled in stone permanently mark Ellen's final resting place.

Roses printed on the cotton of Ellen's dress highlight her quilt block.

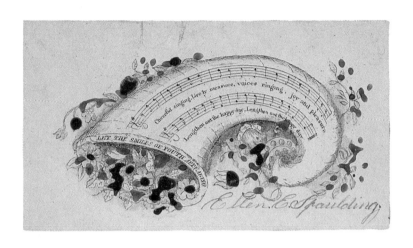

Ellen's stenciled calling cards.

Ellen's bridal friendship quilt,
Album Patch pattern,
by Leonora Spaulding Bagley,
Ludlow, Vermont, 1854,
91 x 96 inches, pieced cottons.

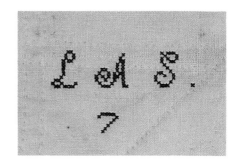

Cross-stitched inventory markings on a cotton pillowcase and sheet used by Leonora for the backing of Ellen's quilt.

Turk Sep 11th 1854

Dear Father and Mother

I have taken my
pen this morning to write you what kind
of a journey we had. We had a very pleasant
time and got along well, we got to Albany
the first night a little before dark and
stoped there to tea, it rained quite hard
when we got there. We got to Buffalo the
next morning where we stopped to breakfast
and that night found us in Toledo where
we had to ferry across the river and then
we went on and got to Chicago the next
noon and when we got there it rained
quite hard, we stopped there a little while
and then went on to Beloit where we all
stoped over night and the next morning
we went on in a stage about twenty
miles to Milton and there we had to stop
till half past eight and then we started
on in the cars again for Madison we got
to Mr Fullers about twelve oclock Saturday

Wistar's Balsam of Wild Cherry

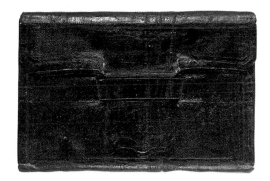

Stedman Spaulding's pocket-size "Book."

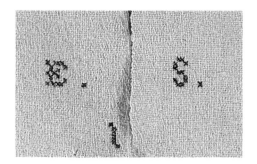

Handspun, handwoven woolen blanket Ellen cross-stitched "E."
and "S." on opposite corners before her marriage.

Part II

Joseph Willard Reed

Willard's mother, six of his half brothers and sisters, and now his wife were all dead and at such young ages. His mother died at twenty-six; Ellen at twenty-two. Since childhood, Willard had grown all too familiar with the pall of death in the house, the coffin in the parlor, the hushed voices. The tall, four-sided gravestone in Chelmsford was etched like a scroll of those he loved:

Lucy E., Aug. 25, 1841. Age, 3 mos.
Caroline A., Feb. 26, 1843. Age, 3 yrs., 3 mos.
Andrew J., Sept. 25, 1844. Age, 6 mos.
Mortimer, Sept. 2, 1845. Age, 1 mo.
Zachery T., Aug. 26, 1848. Age, 7 mos.
Adelaide, Sept. 19, 1850. Age, 6 mos.

Tragically, only four of his stepmother's ten children had survived childhood. Nearly every year there had been a new baby in the household; but from the time Willard was eight, death had followed closely behind the births. Perhaps Willard had come to expect and accept the losses. Death and the ordeal that accompanied it were part of Willard's being, a part of life that he must pass through and over. The year before Willard's birth, his real sister had died at only two months of age. Three years later, his own mother had never recovered from her confinement with her third child, Willard's brother, Charles; she died only six weeks after the birth.

Willard would put Ellen and those gloomy months, those agonizing last days, out of his mind and go on with the work at hand. He had fences to erect, land to clear, barns to build, but he could not erase his belief that he certainly was "no favored child of fortune." All he had to do was to look around himself — there were new babies in almost every family, young boys out in the fields helping their fathers plow, reap, swing the axe. He was already twenty-five years old without even one child to call his own, living or dead. Although he now had many acres of cleared land and a good house, he was at a great disadvantage without a wife, his future bleak and lonely without children to help him. Besides all that, Willard did not like day-to-day living without a woman in the house, and more specifically than that, without Lucy in the house. It was Lucy who had cleaned the floors, washed his pantaloons and shirts, cooked the potatoes, literally kept the fire going that past year. Her presence had comforted Willard on those blistery winter mornings, her tea had warmed him, her smile had cheered him. Had Willard realized then, even as Ellen lay under comfortables in the next room, that he was growing fond of Lucy? Maybe even too fond?

But Ellen was gone now. Seven months had passed already since those grim days when even the landscape had worn the gray mist of grief. Only Stoughton and he now lived in the log house. "We act along very well keeping house," Willard wrote to Stedman on February 12, 1859, without any hint of plans for a drastic change in his life.

Truthfully, Willard was tired of doing housework. Two men in a house just were not the same as a man and a woman. He was as good as any man getting out rails and laying fences, plowing and planting fields, but he could hardly take care of things in the house too, besides having to cook. In less than a month, Willard corrected that. The shocking news of Willard's marriage to Lucy would reach Ellen's parents with their daughter's body still in the storage vault in Ludlow, not yet in a final resting place. It had not been an easy announcement for Willard to make. In fact, he had not known quite how to break the news. Stedman had even paid Lucy the twenty-five dollars for caring for his child all those months. And now Willard had to make a mockery of Lucy's care by marrying her.

Back in Vermont, the long ordeal of the past months had deteriorated Stedman's health. Willard's letter of March 3, 1859, was the final blow to send Stedman to bed under the doctor's care.

Glen Dale   March 3ᵈ, 59

Dear Father & Mother

I write a few lines in answer to yours of Feb 21ˢᵗ   I was sorry to learn that my first letter was not received, for I wrote a long one, and took pains to write much news that I thought would interest you.   the next time I wrote I had time to write but little.   I am sorry to learn that your health is so poor.   I wish you could have stayed here this winter for it has been so mild and pleasant. the snow is gone what little there was   the fields that lay to the South have been bare for two weeks.   the snow has not been so deep as when you left.   we have plenty of hay and I think some to spare.   the cattle colts & shoats are doing well.   the steer was killed a while ago   the weighed nearly six hundred (the meat).   I sold for four dollars a hundred and six cents a pound for the side.   the folks here are all in good health and spirits, and looking forward for better times to come.   I shall send a (Star) [75] with this letter, so that you may see the news, and what is going on at Mauston.   Col Lion [76] has received one or two papers from you   I must not omit to tell you that I was married last week to Lucy Cline.   I got so tired of do-

ing house work, and I thought she would take good care of things in the house. I have not much to write about it only that we live very happily. if married life has many pains, Single life has few pleasures, and it seems a selfish life with nought but one,s self to care for. my sheet is full and I must close. I will write again soon.

ever Yours
J W Reed

Medicine and two pints of whiskey were prescribed for Stedman. He could not write congratulations to Willard. In fact, he would not write to his nephew at all for several months. Then it would be only to tell him that Ellen's last request finally had been carried out. On the 18th of April, the ground was thawed and in such shape that the grave had been dug, and Stedman had quietly witnessed that last step in such an incredibly long ordeal. After nine months of waiting, Ellen rested there, just a short walk up the hill in the serene, silent cemetery nestled in the "old Vermont hills and rocks" she had missed so much. That day Stedman had opened his leather-bound pocket diary (the same one that he had taken to Wisconsin) and written (April) "18th of hay" and on the next line, "Ellen's Remains Burried." [77] He closed the book.

When that news arrived in Glendale, Willard permanently closed the book on Ellen. He was determined that he and Lucy would start anew. He even made plans to build a new house on the other land, at the "Fowler place" on the hill on down the river. Ellen would be forgotten, not mentioned. In addition, by summer there truly was a new beginning for Willard and Lucy. Lucy was in a family way. Hope and joy renewed Willard's spirit. Almost one year to the date of Ellen's burial in Vermont, Willard and Lucy had a new baby in their new house in Plymouth.

Stedman Spaulding's pocket-size "Book."

"Book" opened to entry of Ellen's burial in Ludlow, Vermont.

Once again Stedman and Arterista were totally unprepared for the news they stumbled upon amidst Willard's description of Plymouth and the work he was doing.

Plymouth   April 8th 1860

Dear Father & Mother

I write a few lines to let you know that yours of Feb 15th was received. I have got a house built and am living on the Fowler place. I moved here about the first of March. Stoughton carries on the old place this year. he has got about done sowing wheat by this time & have got in ten acres of wheat & barley here. Sowed it week before last. Should have been done sowing long ago but did not dare to sow oats yet awhile, but shall sow them this week. the ground never was in better order than it is in this Spring. there was no snow on the ground to melt, and there has been no rain of any account. we had the ground all plowed on both farms last fall, and it is a short job to drag it on. There have been two more houses built in sight of here this spring, (Rossman & George Telfer) I can stand in the door and see ten houses, our house in Glen Dale, Ruben Fowlers, and every house between. I have built just on the bank above the field. I am geting out rails to fince the marsh. Stoughton has got out a pile of rails this winter too. I like living off over here very much. my things trouble nobody, and nobody,s things trouble me.   I cannot understand what anybody should wish to live on the road for.   I am handy to the field, to wood & water, to the marsh, and can have a road in any direction by clearing a few logs out of the way, but the worst of it is folks keep coming and sticking themselves under a fellows nose and spoiling all his handy fixings.   there has ten families moved into Glen Dale this Spring, it is geting to be a populous town.   I almost forgot to tell you that we have got a boy at our house, his name is Willard, he is about four weeks old. [78]   Times are hard here at presant, money is scarce, and provisions too, wheat is worth about seven shillings, pork a shilling a pound   I have got some over a hundred bushuls of wheat   I have sold some barley for five shillings. I have to make a payment to Lyon the first of June, and shall keep my wheat as long as I can.   I do not see any chance to sell the place and get any money for it.   if I sell my part [79] I wish to get some money on it so I can buy again.   I should like to get a place fixed up somewhere.   I have got sick of diging grubs and spliting rails and holding breaking plow.   I had rather plow and sow, and gather in the grain.   as I do not think of any thing more to write at present, so I must close

Ever yours
J W Reed

Only one week after the momentous birth of his healthy first son, news of war, of the war between the North and the South, reached the western papers. Even harder, much harder times were ahead. Yet the war was only a shadow as compared to Willard's immediate worries: if he did not raise some money quickly, he would lose his Glendale land, and along with it, all of his thousands of hours of labor and many dollars of expenses. What had been virgin land was now cleared. He had built the poplar log house and barns. He had erected fences to keep in his livestock. All of this he had done in good faith, trusting his "friend" Lyon, who kept insisting he did not need the money. Generous, understanding, sympathetic Lyon. In a matter of months all that had changed. Unfortunately for Willard, the Lyon family held every position in town: lawyer, postmaster, justice of the peace, land speculator, storekeeper....

In November, little Willie was already nine months old, and Willard worried constantly how he would protect his wife and child from the disaster about to befall him. November 6, 1860, was election day. The country was to choose a president, Lincoln or Douglas; yet Willard had other things on his mind. "The boys went to election this afternoon so I came home," Willard wrote to Stedman. "Lyon is crouding up for what is behind on the land up to the old place, it is in fact advertized for sale, I paid four hundred dollars on it last fall, and they promised to wait on me until I could raise it from my crops, but they have altered their minds and think they will have the whole now or the land, and I cannot raise it unless I can have what is coming from Grandsirs estate.[80] I had rather lose my self than to back out from any agreement that I make, but if I do not make out the money it will not only ruin me but others. I should like to have you write immediately and let me know about it."[81]

Certainly Willard was in serious trouble. Not only would he lose his land and four years of breaking ground and planting, but five other people living there (James Neff, Stoughton Haven, his brothers-in-law John and Lewis Cline, as well as Esther) would also lose their property. This was a terribly embarrassing situation, but in truth these friends and family were partially responsible for Willard's dilemma. Lewis and John each owed Willard a large amount of money for the land and had promised to pay by this time. Nevertheless, Willard once again appealed to Stedman for money. This time there was no reply from Ludlow, Vermont.

Willard's letter was dated November 6, 1860. Lyon had initiated foreclosure proceedings nearly a year earlier on February 1, 1859; they had been finalized August 3, 1859, so in truth the land no longer belonged to Willard anyway. Shortly, Willard was officially informed that he had lost his Glendale land. He was devastated, not so much over losing the land, but that someone he trusted had lied to him.

In regard to the land up in Glendale we have lost it it has been such hard times that the rest could not pay me what was due on the land and I could not make it out alone and Lyon has taken advantage of me and made all the cost he could so he has been able to swindle us out of the land and what we have paid on it, but I cannot complain much for it is geting so that the more a man has the worse he is off. taxes are high and then a heavy war tax next Spring that is coming in a hard time to raise money.... if the war tax is as high as some think it will make auful times here. I have got five sheep and we intent to raise enough in time to make our own clothes.[82]

But Willard was still financially dependent on Stedman — after all, Stedman had paid for the land where Willard was living.

Having not heard from his uncle in months, in January Willard once again wrote to Stedman. He desperately needed an answer. "I should like to know something more in regard to the Fowler place, if you intend to let me have it and how and when and all about it, for if I do not have it, I must make some kind of a shift before long." [82]

After such bad troubles, Willard was resigned to most anything, except going to war, but that possibility was becoming more alarming as the days passed. "Wisconsin has raised 18 regiments of infantry besides cavalry and artillery companies, men have left their farms and families," Willard continued in his January 19th letter. "Mauston and Lisbon is full of soldiers. D Little has enlisted and many of the first men of both places."

Adding to Willard's anxiety, Lucy was in a family way again. Only five months later on June 14, 1861, there was a darling baby girl in the Reed house. He and Lucy named her Katie. In that way, Willard's half sister Katie would be remembered. Her death in January of the past year had been so unexpected, such a shock to the entire family. She was only thirteen. [83]

The following October, Willard's younger half brother, twenty-three-year-old George Eaton Reed, enlisted in the army in Massachusetts. [84]   He was "in good spirits, on board Steamer Constitution near Fortress Monroe," when he had last written. [85] Then George was dead; in the army only eight months, never even in a battle — "swamp fever." [86]

It was seven months since Willard had written to Stedman. There had been many changes in that time.

Plymouth, Aug 17th, 1862

Dear Father & Mother

After a long delay I write in answer to yours of Feb 14th. we are all well as usual. we have been well this summer with the exception of about a week in june when we were all sick with the sore throat but we managed to get along and wait upon each other. there has a great many children died with it in this vicinity. some have lost three & four. those that employed all the Doctors they could hear of, lost their children, and the most that used cold water and other simple remedies got well. I had rather have a rattlesnake bite me than to have it again. harvest is nearly ended here. I have one days stacking more to finish. grain is much better than it was last year. the bugs have destroyed many fields of wheat my wheat is not more than half a crop. my barley that I sowed early and put it in well is poor, and that which I sowed late and did not half put it in is good. I half believe that shiftless folks get along best. I have done freting about such things. the poorer I get the richer I feel I have an acre of potatoes close by the house, and three acres of corn up on the Hicks place, that looks well. I have put in 21 acres to crops and shall get it harvested without any help and have cut considerable hay....

There are many going off to war now days I began to think they would have to draft in this county, but when harvest began to draw to a close the quota was was filled and thirteen over. If ever they draft here I expect to go, as I am no favored child of fortune. I do not shrink *from hardships or dangers, but it would be hard for me to leave my family in the situation they would be in were I to leave them. In regard to the place here, it has been a cause of some uneasiness to me. I do not like to lay out a great deal on the land unless I am sure of having it, for it is time to be fixing up a place for a permanant home. I have no fears that if we both live it will be all right but every year that I stay here I am loosing time unless I make considerable improvements on the land.... it costs a great deal of time to get this land subdued. the cost to clear and break an acre on this place will raise three acres of grain on an old farm, but I will write no more. write soon in answer to this.*

*Yours as ever,
J W Reed*

Two weeks later Willard's brother, Charles, had been mustered into the infantry and was already on his way to Washington, then to Fort Monroe. [87] Having just received word of his half-brother George's death, Charles wrote,

It seems rather a hard case for me to go to war but we are afraid if we don't turn out the rebels will get the day, but we don't mean to let them as long as we have a man left.... If God sees fit to let us live nine months, I hope we shall see this terible war settled. [88]

In November of that year, George Reed's personal belongings were sent home to Chelmsford, Massachusetts. A strong man but disheartened father, his one son in the army, another having died in it, his oldest son most likely to be drafted soon, Joseph Reed [89] wrote to Stedman.

Chelmsford Nov. 20th 1862

Brother Stedman

We are a going to send you Georges great coat and some other articles for you to send to Willard. you had better try the coat on   you can tell whether he can wear it or not   if you think he cannot wear it be sure and not send it   we shall put them aboard the cars either saturday or monday by express. We had a letter from Charles to day   he is well   never was better   he says that he has gained fifteen pounds.

we are all well as usual   Maria says she means to write to Willard in a day or two

Very Truely yours   Joseph Reed

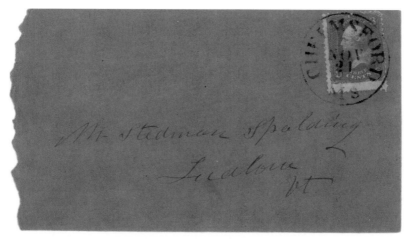

Charles was more fortunate than his half brother George. Having served his nine months of required service without injury or disease, he returned home to Chelmsford on June 3, 1863.

Over a year and a half had passed since Willard last wrote to Stedman and Arterista. Willie had celebrated his fourth birthday only two weeks earlier. Katie would be three in June, and although Willard would not mention it in his letter, Lucy was expecting again. Within several months there would be three little ones in the Reed log house in Plymouth. [90]

Plymouth March 27th,, 64

Dear Father & Mother

It is a long time since I have writen to you and I thought I would write a few lines to let you know that we are all well here except Stoughton,s wife. She is living at our house this winter. The doctor says she has got the liver complaint. Stoughton is up in the pinery.... he thinks he can do better to work out than to cary on a farm. I know that I could for Lucy would nearly take care of herself and the children, and I could save the most of my wages, but I like farming, and I think a man that has a family had better be at home. There is 23 acres broke on the farm. I cary that on and take some land to work besides. I have taken 9 acres of Neff over across the river. I have no one to help me and do not expect to have. I shall sow 30 acres of grain this spring and I expect what I do not harvest with my two hands

159

will go back into the ground, and I have to cut hay for a stock of cattle besides. Wages are very high here, farmers offer $1.00 a day with board. I think they will be $3.00 or $4.00 a day in harvest. this town has not raised a man to fill its quota for the war, and in consequence men are leaving their farms and families by squads and enlisting to fill the quotas of the more wealthy sections of the state for the big bounties rather than run the risk of being drafted. some towns are almost depopulated Glendale has furnished over fifty men and there is only about eighteen left that are liable to the draft if I am drafted I can sholder a musket in two minutes. We called a meeting in this town to raise money for volunteers but could not get a majority. if about half of this town had to go to war I would be willing to go with them just to hear them groan. I am trying to get up another string of fence this spring the snow has been so deep this winter that I did not begin until the middle of Feb. I have choped through all the storms in order to get the fence up before seeding time. I can fence in about 30 acres, (by having a fence on one side) with 160 rods of fence (about 2000 rails) I need a pasture that I can turn in to part of the time, when I am too busy to go after the cows. I have made some of the brush and timber look scared since you was here. I have not broke much but have got some partly cleared so that I can fit it for breaking without much heavy choping. I intend to get a little more broke this season, and next year if I stay here I shall try to break more. I do not feel like laying out much on the place more then my labour, until I have a deed of it. Uncle Sam offers to give a farm to all sons of labor that dare undertake the hardships of the wilderness. I had about as soon go in where it is new once more as not, and if I do the sooner the better....

while I can stay at home I can take care of my family most any where in the wide world but if I have to go to war and get killed or die of disease, they have not much show for geting along in the world. If Lucy could have a deed of the place I should feel better. I wish you would write all about matters and things.

I have letters from Chelmsford frequently. I have got a barrel of flour ready to send home. I shall send you one after harvest if I am not drafted, for I think you must have to pay high prices for your flour, and it will I think be higher next season. every thing that we have to buy is very high here. it takes almost the price of a barrel of flour to buy a pair of boots. we made 25 yds of flanel last fall, and are agoing to make some linen this summer. we get along without buying much. you know it does not cost much to support pride here. I think that I am writing you a good long letter to make up in part for my *negligence* I have not time to write any more now. we send our best wishes to you all.

Ever yours, J. W. Reed.

(write soon)

Lucy Cline Reed

Nine weeks later on June 3, 1864, Lucy was delivered of a daughter. Even as Willard watched his wife gain back her strength, he knew he must soon enlist and go off to the war rather than wait to be drafted. He was thirty-one years old with a wife not very well and three children, Mina less than three months old. It was the worst possible situation, but Willard had no choice. All too soon that dreaded day came when he had to say good-bye, and then trod down that familiar path to the road on his way to Mauston. He had his doubts that he would live to return, that he would ever see Lucy, Willie, Katie, and the baby again. His life thus far had only reinforced his persistent, deep-seated belief that he was "no favored child of fortune."

It was August 22, 1864. Resignedly, Willard signed "Joseph. W. Reed" to the "Volunteer Enlistment" papers.[91] There was no turning back. He had "to take up with the fortunes of a soldier."[92]

The months passed. It was winter now. Willard worried about his wife and the children. They needed him. Lucy's letters only worried him more.

Back in Wisconsin, Lucy did the best she could while her husband was away. She endured the howling, damaging winds that pulled down Willard's fences and ripped shake off the roof; the deep snows that hid the roads and isolated her; the fierce, bitter cold that became terrifying in itself. She endured the lonely, endless nights when she longed for the warmth of Willard's body next to hers. She endured the extreme hardships of the Wisconsin wilderness, and she endured when she and the children struggled to survive the dreaded "sore throat." Depressed, panic-stricken, and feverish herself, Lucy nursed her children through the days and nights, remembering three years earlier when a "great many children died" of it. At that time Willard and she, and the children, had recovered by avoiding doctors and by using "cold water and other simple remedies."

So Lucy endured alone, day after day throughout the numerous crises, but the worst of it was never knowing whether her husband was still alive. Way out in Wisconsin, news was very scarce. She would hear word of a huge battle and then there would only be silence. At times the anxiety would become so intense that it was not uncommon for a neighbor woman to set out at night while her children slept, "through deep woods lighted by a tallow candle enclosed in a tin can punched full of holes to Col. Lyon's store for news of their men folk."[93]

The beginning of the new year, Willard penned a letter to Stedman and Arterista.

Camp Butler,   Jan 10th, 65

Dear Father & Mother,

As it is some time since I have writen to you, I I thought I would write a few lines to let you know that I am in good health and spirits, and hope these few lines will find you all in the enjoyment of the same blessing. I have been here in this Camp since the last of October for the most of the time. I have enjoyed the best of health all the while that I have been in the service. the members of our Co are mostly a fine lot of men, and I get along with soldiering far better than I expected. The right wing of the Regiment is still at Cairo, the left is scattered about over this state, one Co in a place. Besides doing guard duty we are going all the while to escort men to various points at the South & West. it is but a few days since I got back from a trip to Nashville, and New York city. About twenty five of our Co went with me, we took two hundred substitutes and drafted men down to Nashville. they were assigned to regiments in Sherman,s army. when we got there they would not receive them, but sent us on to New York with them, so we had quite a trip. we were gone fifteen days, and traveled about three thousand miles. I was very much disappointed in the appearance of the country through Kentucky. the soil looked poor, the buildings did not look thrifty, the stations along the railroad were small and scattering. As we were going down we met several trains of rebel prisoners coming north. As we stoped on a switch opposite one of the trains some of the rebels began to beg for bread. our boys passed out all the hard tack and meat that they had saying ,,you will get enough to eat up north ,, Uncle Sam has got a plenty for you etc,, one of the boys as he handed out a handful of hard tack asked them if they could not hur- rah for Old Abe. I could not help thinking of Libby Prison and the Pen at Andersonville. I cannot write a very long letter this time as we have orders to get ready to go to Cairo. I get letters from Chelmsford frequently. they were all well at the last accounts Lucys health is not very good this winter. she and the children have been sick with the sore throat. I should like very much to see them, but I must take up with the fortunes of a soldier and try to be content. my sheet is nearly full and I must close. write soon. direct letters to Camp Butler, Ill. and the letters will follow the Reg.

I remain yours, J. W. Reed

Contrary to his gut feelings, in the most critical of all cir- cumstances, Willard proved indeed he *was* a "favored child of for- tune" after all. The war over, he was discharged at Madison, Wisconsin, on June 20, 1865. Willard soon boarded the train headed for home. For ten months he had not seen Lucy, little Willie, Katie, or Mina; however, the sights his eyes took in as he walked down that last stretch of road from the Fowlers' shocked him and dampened his joy — fields unplowed, unplanted, overgrown; rails of fencing down in all kinds of configurations. There was unending work to be done everywhere he looked and it was already summer, far too late in the season to catch up. He knew they were in for the hardest year of all.

Once more Willard started in with axe and plow.

Part III

Lathrop, Missouri
1875

"Tell George we wish he would appear to us as he did once before...." [94] Ellen had written that message on the top edge of a letter in 1857, concerning her cousin George Alden Patch, the only son of Stedman's older sister, Sally. (Sally Spaulding Patch had died in 1860 and was the first to be buried in the cemetery plot with Ellen. George's father, Alden, and Stedman continued their partnership in the gristmill next to the Spaulding brick home in Ludlow until Alden's sudden death in 1869.) For years George seemed to wander around the country, always returning to Cavendish, Vermont, where he married Emma —. Finally in 1866, his wife pregnant with their first child, George had decided to settle in Lathrop, Missouri, a new site for a station for the Hannibal and St. Joseph Railroad. There he took the job as station agent [95] with "some twenty trains passing...in a day with cattle hogs mules corn flour and wheat to St. Luis or Chicago five or six at a time." [96]

In the winter of 1875, George became very ill and was unable to work at the depot, and even more seriously, unable to carry

George Alden Patch   Emma Patch

on his farm. Besides that, grasshoppers were ravaging the land along the Mississippi River and migrating towards Clinton County. George was in a desperate situation. Without help he would soon lose all of his crops. His only solution appeared to be his cousin J. Willard Reed in Wisconsin. He would write and appeal to Willard to assist him for a few months.

Almost ten years had passed since Willard's return from the war, ten years of back-breaking toil; and yet, he never seemed to get ahead. He was forty-two, his three children growing up. Willie was already fifteen, certainly a great help to him; still Willard was weary trying to "subdue the land." It had taken years of labor and disappointments, even heartache, to break Willard's spirit, but he had grown discouraged, even given up the idea of getting rich in the West. Maybe now he could hear Ellen's voice in his head, her whining, her begging, her all consuming desire to quit, to sell out, to go home to New England where they could have things nice, where they could have familiar faces around them, instead of weeks-old ink on paper. It had taken Willard twenty years, but he had finally come to the same conclusion, the same desire. The previous fall he had journeyed back to Chelmsford, Massachusetts, because Maria, his stepmother, was gravely ill. She died in February at sixty one years of age. While in New England, he had also gone up to Ludlow to visit with Stedman and Arterista. In twenty years New England had changed; familiar faces had changed even more. His "mother" was gone; his father aged. Willard decided to sell everything in Plymouth, Wisconsin. He was going to take his family "home."

But fate was not to permit Willard to carry out his plans. George Patch's persuasive letter arrived in Plymouth, Wisconsin. Only a folded piece of paper with ink, that letter would change the course of Willard's life. Willard's decision to help his cousin marked the beginning of the rest of his life.

In May, Willard wrote to Stedman and Arterista.

Lathrop, May 23ᵈ 1875.

Dear Father & Mother
        I take the present time to write a few words
to let you know how we are geting along at present, and
how the times and prospects are here in Missourie. George
seems to be improving, is able to look after his business, but
think that he does not gain strength as he ought to. we
are just in the edge of the grasshopper region, their
depradations seem to be confined to three tiers of counties
along the Missourie River, one in Kansas and two in
this state, they seem to be in spots in this vicinity. there
were lots of them hatched out between George,s house and
the depot, while on the other side and on out to George,s
farm there are but very few, on some farms they are eat-
ing up everything, on other farms there are none at all, but
in the next county South they are taking everything clean.
some farmers here have not planted their corn, are holding
on to their seed, think that by the middle of June the
hoppers will take wing and leave, as they did nine years
ago, and folks here say that they can raise a crop of corn
after that time. a drove of cattle went by here last week
driven out away from the hoppers to keep them from
starving. I have not much of an idea what George will

170

do if his crops are destroyed this season. I shall do everything that I can for him now that I am here. thought it was a foolish move for us both in my coming, but George would not take no for an answer, was going to lose so much if I did not come and assist him, so I thought that if such was the case that I would make a sacrifice and come at all hazard. I hope for the best. I wanted to fix up our farm in Plymouth this season and sell it this fall and go back East, and now I do not have much of an idea how things are coming arround. I told George jokingly this morning that if everything was destroyed here, horses would be cheap and I could rig up a team and start back to Wisconsin overland, stop along the road and help folks do up their work, and get up to Minnesota and help harvest their grain. we have old friends and neighbours scattered along all the way from Storm Lake in Iowa to the Mississippi. we could go on a regular visiting tour. we all want to see you here very much. George is confident that you will be here soon, but I cannot make it seem as though you will come before fall. I want you to write soon as you get this all about everything, when you are coming and if you hear anything about the folks at Chelmsford coming out. Lucien has sold out his milk route and is now at home. Father had gone up country with cattle as usual. Katie is going to school. they all seem to be geting along nicely at home....[97]

171

I think often of the pleasant visit I had with you all last fall, and regret that I could not have remained longer with you, but hope to again meet you all at no very distant day. George is writing to Leonora to day. give our respects to her and Thomas and children..... shall not tell you how I like this country for I hardly know myself. the fears of grasshopper plague seem to cast a shadow of gloom over the whole of this fertile region....

Lucy,s health is about as usual. Minnie goes to school, likes her school very much. Willie works with me on the farm, has drove George,s team almost every day since we have been here. I want to have things grow here this season very much. it does not seem as though I was ever half so anxious when I farmed for myself, but we can only work and wait. As I do not think of anything more I will close hoping to hear from you soon.

Willard began to like Lathrop more than he had expected. He really did go back to Plymouth and sell out, but not to move back east as he had thought. Instead, the year 1878 found Willard, Lucy, Willie, Katie, and Minnie living in Lathrop, Missouri, "a half mile East of George,s at the south east corner of the Village." And in October of that year Stedman and Willard's brother, Charles, came to visit. It was "very dark when [they got] off the Car at the Depot." George and his wife, and Willard and Willie were there on the platform to meet them. "Lathrop is a large Village," Stedman wrote to his wife. "The houses are spred over a large teritory it is pretty level and they have plenty of room.... I think this is a

Postal card from Stedman Spaulding to his wife from Lathrop, Missouri, on November 24, 1878: "Dear Wife I am here in Lathrop yet I have stayed much longer here than I intended to stay....

beautiful looking place as good as any I have seen since I left home." [98]   "The Village is thinly settled a good many houses and a good ways apart not much like Ludlow." [99]   Stedman and Charles had a good, long visit; they stayed one whole month.

Three years passed. "Willard is farming, and peddling milk — He started last winter and for some months carried his milk round twice a day in his hands, but that was too much for any one to do, so he bought him a top buggy and takes one verry large can and some smaller ones in that which is much easier — They are all well," [100]   continued George Patch in late August of 1881.

Five months later on February 2, 1882, Ellen's mother, Arterista Haven Spaulding, died. Stedman and she had been married fifty-one years; he took her death very hard.

Leonora's youngest child, Ellen, came to stay with Stedman, to keep house and to keep him company. "We were glad to learn that you was comparatively well and that Ellen is with you — We can well immagine your lonliness, and wish that you both would come here and stay with us as long as you could —" George Patch wrote.

About life in Missouri, he continued, "Willard is milking cows and pedling milk — I have rented him about forty acres of my farm, which Will has plowed and planted in corn — Katie is teaching school about two miles from home." [101] It was May of 1882. Willard would be fifty the following year. Brunette, brown-eyed Katie would be celebrating her twenty-first birthday in another month. Perhaps Willard thought of how young his daughter seemed, how young she really was, and that his first wife, Ellen, had died at only twenty-two.

But the differences between the two were dramatic. Katie was a true western girl. She had never lived any place other than the Western Country. She was born in a log house in the densely wooded valley of the Baraboo River in the difficult times of the Civil War. When Katie was only three, her father had departed to go off to war leaving her mother alone with her, her four-year-old brother, Willie, and baby sister, Minnie. Life was hard then and for years to follow.

Ever since Katie was a little girl, her mother always complained of never being well. Katie had taken over many of the household tasks, and she accepted as a matter-of-fact the daily hardships of living out west, the never-ending struggle to survive against the greatest of adversity.

Unlike Ellen, Katie had never become accustomed to nice things. For years she wore homespun dresses and petticoats of flannel or coarser woven wools from the fleece of her father's sheep, or of tow or linen from the flax her father had planted. And the quilts, "comfortables," and blankets were not pieced out of pretty printed cottons as Ellen's, but instead were from homespun. They were simply for warmth, for survival against the severe Wisconsin winters. No new factory-woven cloth could be purchased for a quilt top or quilt back when money was so scarce. As her father always said, "It does not cost much to support pride here." But when Katie was ten, her family had moved to Lathrop, and her life gradually became easier. At twenty, she began teaching school.

Katie Reed

Minnie has got to be quite a girl; is over eighteen years old but small for her age. Mothers health is about the same as usual, never very good you know, but with the help of Minnie she is able to do all the work.

Lathrop, Missouri, June. 12. 1882.

Dear Uncle Steadman:

We received a letter from you some time ago, but don't beleive father has answered it yet, and thinking you might like to hear from us I will write you a few lines this evening. Am teaching school out here about three miles from town, have been teaching two months and have another month to teach. I have a nice little school of twenty eight scholars and I enjoy the work ever so much. Am boarding with some very pleasant people, (quite recently from New York,) who live about seven minutes walk from the school house. I go home Friday evening and come out here Sunday eve.

The folks at home were quite well with the exception of Will; his lungs have been troubling him for some time, and I fear they are in a bad condition. He looks real miserable and coughs a great deal. We feel quite anxious about him. Father is very busy now. He supplies the town with milk, has all the care of the cows besides delivering the milk. He gets up real early and keeps at work most of the time. He is talking of hiring a man and I hope he will, for he is working too hard. George Patch is going into the milk business in Kansas City....

I wish you could see this country now: It is more beautiful than at any other time.

The prospect, for an abundance of peaches and apples, is very good. We had so little of fruit last year that we will fully appreciate it when we do have it....

We were hoping that you would be able to come out and spend the summer with us. I think it would do you good if you could, and we would like so much to have you. It must indeed be very lonely for you since Aunt's death, and we all deeply sympathise with you in your terrible bereavement, but can only point you to that great comforter who can "wipe away all tears from our eyes."

Katie finished her letter across the top of the inside pages, her closing written lengthwise on them:

I have not written you all I wanted but my sheat is full and it is real late so I must close. We shall hope to hear from you before long.
Yours affectionately Katie M. Reed.
Good night.

Willard and Lucy had tried to forget Ellen. They had never mentioned her to their children; yet now they had a constant reminder of those dark days when they had gotten to know one another. Ellen had been twenty-two; now Willie, the same age, had a cough that refused to go away.

But the story was not the same this time. Willie recovered. And two years later, he was not only married and working in his father's creamery, but Katie also had exciting plans:

Willie Reed

My school closed in January and I suppose it is my last school as I will marry (next September) a young man named Albert McWilliams. He is a merchant in Turney (the next station north of here) and is a splendid fellow, honest upright and better than all, is a true christian. We are to be married the tenth of Sep. and start immediately for Ohio on a three weeks visit to his relatives. We will live in Turney which is on the rail road and only seven miles from here which will be very pleasant as I can see my folks very often, Oh! life seems so bright and happy to me now, and the future seems much brighter.[102]

Perhaps that letter of Katie's sounded familiar to Stedman Spaulding. Even though thirty years had passed, undoubtedly he remembered another happy young woman excitedly preparing to be married, all of her future looming brightly before her, too. Willard's daughter, Katie, was to be married September 10, 1884 — the same month and thirty years almost to the day of Ellen and Willard's wedding.

For Katie, that date of September 5, 1854, held no special significance. Her father's marriage to Ellen was never mentioned. Back in Vermont, however, Ellen's sister, Leonora, remembered that day, and she had Ellen's cherished wedding present, Ellen's bridal friendship quilt, as tangible proof. In 1854, each stitch had been made with hopes for Ellen's bright future. Each inscribed name represented the wishes of a loved one for her happiness.

In those last hours when she finally had to face the reality of death, Ellen Spaulding Reed had wanted to leave something of herself so that she would not be forgotten. After nearly four years in the West, she did not have many possessions, and even fewer of any value. But she did have treasures to pass on that were more meaningful than all else. She had the work of her hands, the quilts that she herself had pieced and quilted from the cloth of the people and places she had lived. And she had her bridal friendship quilt, Leonora's gift to her so many years earlier.

"I am pieceing me a comfortable, called Boneparts re-treat," [103] she had written two years before her death. But that was not the only quilt she had made; there were more. In those last dramatic hours of her life, she had been very specific regarding her wishes: first, concerning where she would be buried; second, to whom her quilts should be given. She wanted her parents to give several quilts to Willard's parents, and one to her husband's brother and his wife, Charles and Emily. Of course, she wanted her parents to keep one for themselves. Her most meaningful quilt of all, her bridal friendship quilt, she willed back to Leonora.

Ellen's parents faithfully carried out her wishes. Willard's father, Joseph Reed, included a "thank-you" note in his letter nearly two years after Ellen's death.

Charles and Emily Reed's home at 156 North Road, Chelmsford, Massachusetts, originally built by Emily's father at the time of their marriage. Carrying out one of Ellen's last requests, Stedman and Arterista mailed the designated quilt to this house.

Ellens quilts came safe and were very gladly received by us and also Charles and Emily rec'd thiers with great pleasure. I do not think of any thing more now and Mrs Reed will finish.

Dear Friends
we received Ellens kind presant and feel very much pleased with them and feell very greatful to you for your trouble and hope I can repay you sometime.

Maria E. Reed [104]

Maria E. Reed

Epilogue

On April 14, 1885, one day before his eighty-first birthday, Stedman Spaulding died "seized." In the tradition of the times, Leonora ordered a silver coffin plate etched with lilies of the valley encircling her father's name:

Mr Stedman Spaulding.
Died April 14 -1885.
Aged 81 Years.

In the final three years of his life, Stedman had spoken the name "Ellen" many times each day. It was *Ellen* who poured his afternoon tea, brought him his letters, baked him ginger snap cookies. But it was not his daughter Ellen; it was his granddaughter Ellen Mary who lived with him, his companion during his last years.

When Ellen Mary first began helping him, she was nearly twenty-one; just before Stedman died, she celebrated her twenty-third birthday. Ironically, those were the years Stedman had missed with his own daughter. Perhaps at times it was difficult for Stedman to say the name "Ellen"; perhaps in his old age he had glimpses of his own daughter Ellen. At least in those years without Arterista by his side, he had come to know some of the loneliness that had consumed his daughter in her last years. "Very dark and lonely to me here a lone," he penned into his diary from inside the brick house in Ludlow, Vermont.[105]

Certainly Stedman never forgot his daughter. His box of her

letters was proof. For over a quarter of a century Stedman saved those letters. After Stedman's passing, Leonora also saved and cherished her father's box of letters containing Ellen's cheerful first letters as a new bride, to her gloomy last letters of hopelessness and isolation, and then Stedman's letter to Leonora conveying the dreaded news of her sister's death. That letter had arrived days after Ellen's funeral in Wisconsin. Leonora had mourned in silence. But less than three years later, she gave birth to a baby girl, and in memory of her sister, Leonora named the child "Ellen."

So it was this child, Leonora's unmarried daughter, Ellen Mary, who cared for Stedman in his last years and who lived in the brick house after his death. Tragically, like her aunt, Ellen Mary died prematurely at only forty-one years of age. The funeral was held in the parlor of the Spaulding brick house. Leonora was there standing by the coffin in the very house where she and her sister, Ellen, had enjoyed their youth, the house to which her sister had longed to return. And soon, Ellen Mary would join Ellen in the graveyard on the quiet hillside above that house.

With Leonora's death nine years later in 1912, her son Fred and his wife, Kate, were the ones left to protect Ellen Spaulding Reed's letters and bridal friendship quilt, passing them on to their only son, Warren. In time the quilt became known as "Leonora's quilt." Toward the end of his life, Warren gave "Leonora's quilt" to his mother's sister, his aunt Helen J. Barton, who lived with him. Warren died in 1965.

The story of the quilt had been forgotten, the life of Ellen, too. Needing money at the end of her life, Mrs. Barton asked her daughter Barbara Barton Chiolino to sell the quilt for her. Once again Ellen's quilt made a western journey, only this time to California where Linda Otto Lipsett discovered it. She then began her

Fred Bagley   Kate Bagley

search for the story of this friendship quilt. The only information she had was that on the quilt itself — the names and places on the front and the cross-stitched initials "L.A.S." on the backing. Several years later she located a will of a descendant of the quiltmaker — Warren Bagley. He had left everything to Mrs. Helen J. Barton. Her phone number was in the Ludlow, Vermont, telephone directory. Her daughter Barbara Barton Chiolino had a box of letters she kept because of the stamps on the envelopes. She said she would begin reading them. Maybe they would tell something of the story of the names on the friendship quilt....

Scrap Bag

Pieces of Their Lives

Lucy Cline Reed and her granddaughter
Madge Bennett (Mina's daughter).

Condensed Family History

Lucy J. Cline was born in <u>Fairfax, Franklin Co. Vt.</u> on Feb. 15, 1839. They were married on Feb. 22, 1859 at Glendale, Monroe Co. Wis. Willard W. was married in Camden on Dec. 6, 1883 to Stella Young of Camden N.Y. Katie M. was married in Lathrop on Sept. 10, 1884 to Albert McWilliams of Turney, Mo. Mina J. married June 3, 1885 at Lathrop to James L. Bennett of Turney, Mo. — Three Children ....

Joseph [Willard] Reed died at Austin May 13, 1911.... Lucy Reed died at Adrian Mar. 24, 1930. Mina [Reed] Bennett at Sedalia Nov. 6, 1930. Willard W. Reed died at Branson Oct. 16, 1931. Albert McWilliams died at Adrian Feb. 23, 1933.

From two very old, typed pages of Joseph Willard Reed's family genealogy found at the home of Harland McWilliams, great-grandson of J. Willard Reed.

Mrs. Katie McWilliams Dead

Mrs. Katie McWilliams, 85 years old, died in a convalescent home in Kansas City, Kansas, Sunday, January 27, 1946. Mrs. McWilliams had moved to Kansas City about two years ago to be near her sons. Previous to that time she had lived in Adrian and Archie.

Katie M. Reed was united in marriage to Albert A. McWilliams at Plattsburg, Missouri, September 10, 1884. To this union three sons were born, Dr. Cline V., DeWitt and Lucien McWilliams, all of Kansas City. Mr. McWilliams died while the family lived in Adrian, February 22, 1933....

The Adrian Journal, Adrian, Missouri, Thursday, Jan. 31, 1946.

Sad News. — T.C. Bagley was the recipient, Wednesday, of the sad news that his sister, Mrs. L. Cline, perished in the terrible prairie fire that ravaged Douglass County, Dak., April 2d. The details of the tragedy, as given by the local paper, are as follows:

Mr. Cline and wife were alone on the farm when the fire was first seen. He attempted to save the stock and ran to help his wife. He went to every room but one, calling her, and finally concluded she had gone to the cave. The fire was by this time between him and the cave, and he ran for the "fire break." The supposition is that Mrs. Cline, overcome by fright, fainted and perished in the house, in the only room her husband had failed to enter in his search, and which they were not in the habit of frequenting. Both Mr. Cline and his son lost all their farm buildings and stock, being the heaviest losers in that vicinity.

Found in Katie Reed's scrapbook. Although the year of Esther's death was not included, she died just prior to 1900. In the 1900 census, her husband, Lewis, was seventy-seven years old and living with their son Edgar and his family in Chester Township, Douglas County, South Dakota. Edgar, only about six in 1857 when they had lived in the shanty with Ellen Spaulding Reed, was now listed as a lawyer. He and his wife, Fanny, had two children: twelve-year-old Howard and eight-year-old Esther.

Death of Ellen M. Bagley.

Miss Ellen M. Bagley was born at Reading March 26, 1861. The larger portion of her life was spent in the town of Ludlow. She was a devoted member of the Methodist Episcopal church for many years....

For some time she had been in feeble health and on Dec. 25th died at her home on Main street. Funeral services were held at the home, Rev. X.M. Fowler officiating.

By her own request, Walter Baker, Warren Bagley, William Bagley and Robert Bagley, her nephews, acted as pallbearers.

She leaves an aged mother to whom she was especially devoted, a sister and two brothers to mourn her loss.

The grape is trodden in the press
    To yield the quickening wine
And souls by sorrow only, win
    The brotherhood Divine.

There is no death save fear of death;
    The soul that once is free
Shall find behind the veil of Time
    But larger liberty.

Then will I, Lord, await the end
    With no unfilial dread,
And listen for Thy voice to call
    The Living from the Dead.

Newspaper clipping found in Katie Reed's scrapbook.

Leonora A. Spaulding Bagley

Leonora Spaulding Bagley died at eighty years of age on October 11, 1912, of "pernicious anaemia." Her husband, Thomas Curtis Bagley, had died ten years earlier almost to the day, on October 4, 1902, age seventy. At the time of her death, Leonora was living with her daughter Ella (Oella A.) and Ella's husband, William Litchfield. Upon the settlement of Leonora's estate, Ella received "$238.50 in full payment for board and care" of her mother. Leonora's son Fred took care of all of the funeral and burial arrangements and was executor of the estate. Two of Leonora's five children had died before her: Ellen, and Leonora's second son, James, who died in 1899 at forty-seven years of age. Leonora's youngest son, Frederick Herbert, born December 19, 1856, married Catherine (Kate) Sawyer, August 10, 1878, and had three children. Two of them died in infancy. Only Warren, the heir of Ellen's quilt, lived a full life and died in 1965.

Leonora's son Fred seated on the barrel inside gristmill attached to the Spaulding brick house.

From Kate and Warren Bagley's Cookbook

Ellen Bagley's Ginger Snaps

1 cup of butter

1 cup of molasses

1 cup of sugar

1/2 cup of sweet milk

2 teaspoons of soda

1 teaspoon of ginger

Note: Add the necessary flour
        for rolling out.

Ellen's Ginger Bread

1 cup of sour milk

1 cup of molasses

1/2 cup of butter

1 egg

1 teaspoon of soda

1 teaspoon of ginger

Add necessary flour

Ellen's Pickled Blackberries

7 pounds of berries

4 pounds of sugar

1 1/2 pints of vinegar

1 teaspoon of cloves, cinnamon, ginger and mace, each

Boil 20 minutes.

Inscriptions on Ellen's Quilt

Note: On the quilt each part of the name and place have been decorated, or punctuated, with flourishes of the pen like double commas and quotation marks (see Ellen's block p. 130). Those have been omitted from the following list.

Row A

1	Lucy Ann Hubbard	Reading
2	Emily A Haven	Ludlow
3	Delorma C Bagley	Cavendish Vt
4	Ellen E Reed	Ludlow Vt
5	Sarah E Hubbard	Reading

Row B

6	Maria L Reed	Chelmsford Mass
7	Cornelia M Haven	Ludlow Vt
8	Lorenda Parker	Cavendish Vt
9	Mrs M Reed	Chelmsford Mass

Row C

10	Mr S Spaulding	Ludlow Vt
11	Mary E Hall	Reading Vt
12	George A Patch	Ludlow Vt
13	Mrs A S Hall	Reding Vt.
14	J Willard Reed	Burke Wiss

Row D

15	Mrs L Haven	Ludlow Vt
16	Mrs L Reed	Chelmsford Mass
17	Mrs M Proctor	Cavendish
18	Mr J Haven	Ludlow Vt

Row E

19	Mr R C Haven	Ludlow Vt
20	Mr T C Bagley	Reading Vt
21	Helen H Hubbard	Reading Vt
22	Austin C Bagley	Reading Vt
23	Prescott R Haven	Ludlow Vt

Row F

24	Sarah P Haven	Ludlow Vt
25	Stoughton A Haven	Ludlow Vt
26	Ivory R Haven	Ludlow Vt
27	Mr A Patch	Ludlow Vt

Row G

28	Mrs S Patch	Ludlow Vt
29	James P Bagley	Pawlet Vt
30	Mrs L M Page	Warrenton Vt
31	Catharine S Reed	Chelmsford Mass
32	Sumner J Haven	Ludlow Vt

Row H

33	Mrs M F Bagley	Pawlet Vt
34	Mrs E Cline	St Albans Bay Vt
35	Mrs L A Bagley	Reading Vt
36	Mr J Bagley	Pawlet Vt

Row I

37	Mr and Mrs A Spaulding	Cavendish Vt
38	James S Bagley	Reading Vt
39	Mrs S Crawford	Pawlet Vt
40	N Lovina Keyes	Cavendish
41	Mary H Bagley	Pawlet Vt

Row J

42	Harriet Proctor	Cavendish Vt
43	Sarah L Spaulding	Cavendish Vt
44	Mrs C Works	Cavendish Vt
45	Mrs A Spaulding	Ludlow Vt

a	Roxanna Spaulding	Reading
b	Mrs A Wheelor	Reading
c	Mrs L E Haven	Ludlow Vt.
d	Roxanna Spaulding	Cavendish Vt
e	Mrs Hubbard	Reading
f	Mary L Riggs	Ludlow
g	Lorenda Parker	Cavendish
h	Julia M Adams	
i	Mrs Julia Hager	Cavendish
j	Mrs D Spaulding	Cavendish
k		Cavendish Vt
l	Eliza A Earl	Ludlow
m	S Eveline Witherell	Reading
n	Olive Sawyer	Nashua
o	Mrs A Blanchard	Cavendish
p	Martha A Russell	Cavendish
q	Ann Sawyer	Ludlow
r	Mrs B Proctor	Cavendish
s	Marcella Parker	Cavendish
t	Lucy Sawyer	Nashua
u	Mrs C Spaulding	Reading

A — J	Vertically
1 — 45	Horizontally from left to right
a — u	Clockwise around the outer edges

In the summer of 1854 at the time the quilt was signed...

1 Lucy Ann Hubbard	13	Neighbor of Leonora in Reading
2 Emily A. Haven*	10	Cousin
3 Delorma C. Bagley*	33	Leonora's brother-in-law
4 **Ellen E. Reed**	19	
5 Sarah E. Hubbard	12	Neighbor of Leonora in Reading
6 Maria L. Reed*	17	Cousin, half sister of Ellen's future husband
7 Cornelia M. Haven	6	Cousin
8 Lorenda Parker	16	From Ohio, living with relatives Betsey and Amos Proctor
9 **Mrs M Reed** **[Maria]**	41	Aunt, future stepmother-in-law of Ellen
10 **Mr S Spaulding** **[Stedman]**	50	Father
11 Mary E Hall*	35	Neighbor of Leonora in Reading
12 **George A. Patch**	21	Cousin
13 Mrs A S Hall [Anna]	64	Neighbor of Leonora in Reading
14 **J. Willard Reed**	21	Cousin, future husband
15 **Mrs L Haven** **[Lydia Coleman]**	68	Grandmother, a quilter
16 Mrs L Reed [Leonora]	Deceased	Aunt and the mother of J. Willard Reed
17 Mrs M Proctor [Maria E.]	24	Second cousin
18 **Mr J [James] Haven**	69	Grandfather
19 Mr R C Haven* [Ryland C.]	44	Uncle
20 **Mr T C Bagley** **[Thomas Curtis]**	22	Brother-in-law, husband of Leonora
21 Helen H Hubbard	22	Neighbor of Leonora in Reading

22 Austin C Bagley*	4	Nephew, sister's child
23 Prescott R Haven	18	Cousin
24 Sarah P Haven	9	Cousin
25 **Stoughton A Haven**	18	Cousin
26 **Ivory R Haven**	20	Cousin
27 Mr A [Alden] Patch*	54	Uncle
28 Mrs S [Sally] Patch*	55	Aunt
29 James P Bagley	28	Sister's brother-in-law
30 Mrs L M Page		
31 Catharine A Reed*	8	Cousin, half sister of J. Willard Reed
32 Sumner J Haven	17	Cousin
33 Mrs M F Bagley* [Mary F.]		Sister's mother-in-law
34 **Mrs E Cline** [**Esther Pitcher Bagley**]	27	Sister's sister-in-law, Ellen's close friend
35 **Mrs L A Bagley** [**Leonora A.**]	**22**	**Sister, the quiltmaker**
36 Mr J [James] Bagley		Sister's father-in-law
37 **Mr and Mrs A Spaulding** [**Asa and Rhoda White**]		Grandparents; grandmother died in 1848
38 James S Bagley*	2	Nephew, sister's child
39 Mrs S Crawford		
40 N Lovina Keyes*	19	Friend
41 Mary H Bagley*		Leonora's sister-in-law, friend
42 Harriet Proctor	13	Relative
43 Sarah L Spaulding*	27	Second cousin
44 Mrs C Works [Carlista P.]	24	Friend
45 **Mrs A Spaulding** [**Arterista**]	41	Mother

a Roxanna Spaulding	19	Neighbor of Leonora in Reading, also a relative, living with John and Anna Wheeler in 1850 census
b Mrs A Wheelor* [Anna]	61	Neighbor of Leonora in Reading Note: She died July 9, 1854. Her block was probably signed before her death.
c Mrs L E Haven* [Lucy Eaton]	46	Aunt, Second wife of Ryland C.
d Roxanna Spaulding	19	Same as block #a. She is living in Reading, but her real home is in Cavendish.
e Mrs [Mary] Hubbard	47	Neighbor of Leonora in Reading
f Mary L Riggs*	18	Friend, niece of Ryland Haven's first wife
g Lorenda Parker		Same as block # 8
h Julia M Adams	33	Friend
i Mrs Julia Hager	32	Wife of the mechanic in Cavendish
j Mrs D Spaulding [Dolly]	53	Second cousin's wife
k		Town listed only
l Eliza A Earl	10	Friend, father is a shoemaker
m Eveline Witherell	27	Neighbor of Leonora in Reading
n Olive Sawyer	20	Friend
o Mrs A Blanchard [Augusta]	36	Friend, husband is a shoemaker
p Martha A Russell	14	Friend
q Ann Sawyer	59	Friend of the family
r Mrs B [Betsey] Proctor	59	Relative
s Marcella Parker	18	From Ohio, living with the Proctors
t Lucy Sawyer	22	Friend
u Mrs C Spaulding [Catherine]	24	Probably a relative, neighbor of Leonora in Reading

Names in **bold** print denote principle people in the book.

* Denotes persons Ellen Spaulding Reed mentioned in her letters.

Ages are for the year of 1854 gathered from census and vital records.

Footnotes

[1] Each of the pillowcases is identical with L.A.S 6 one-quarter of an inch high in a fine, bronze-colored silk thread, the lettering tiny and similar to that on early samplers. The cross-stitched initials on the sheet are different: the letters are in a fancier script, about nine-sixteenths of an inch tall in a fine, black, cotton thread. It is possible that the pillowcases were part of Willard's mother's trousseau, saved after her young death in 1835, and used for Ellen's quilt. Her maiden name was Leonora Spaulding, as was Ellen's sister's maiden name. All known records, including her gravestone, however, list her name as Leonora Spaulding Reed. A middle initial, if she did have one, has been dropped (quilt block #16).

Initialing and numbering linens was a standard practice at this time. A pair of sheets and a matching pair of pillowcases would have the same number so that they could be laundered in rotation to insure equal wear. Also in large family or community washings, a woman could easily identify her own linens.

[2] Conflicting records record William White's death as February 21 or March 14, 1621. (*Ancestral Chronological Record of the William White Family*, p. 24.)

Governor Bradford only wrote that "Mr. White and his two servants died soon after their landing." (Kellogg, *Mayflower Families Through Five Generations*, p. 95.)

[3] William and Susanna White were the parents of Peregrine White, "the first Englishman born in New England."

On Monday, December 4, 1620, while men were sent out on a "discovery" expedition, "it pleased GOD that Mistress White was brought to bed of a son; which was called "PEREGRINE." (Arber, *The Story of The Pilgrim Fathers*, pp. 104, 426.)

[4] The exact date of birth is unknown at this time. Until 1857, one did not have to file birth, marriage, or death records in the state of Vermont. The first birth record filed by Leonora and Thomas Bagley was for their fourth child, Frederick, born December 19, 1856, and recorded in 1857.

[5] In his diary Stedman reversed Willard's name by mistake. Stedman had arrived at George Spaulding's in Burke, Wisconsin, on September 1, 1854, and stayed there until September 4.

[6] Ellen E. Reed to Stedman and Arterista Spaulding, from Burke, Wisconsin to Ludlow, Vermont, April 1, 1855.

[7] On the day of Ellen's wedding, Stedman was traveling home by stage and train and passed through Milton, Wisconsin.

8 Ellen E. Reed to Stedman and Arterista Spaulding, from Burke, Wisconsin to Ludlow, Vermont, September 11, 1854.

9 John Lewis Peyton described Chicago in the 1850's as having "no pavement, no macadamized streets, no drainage." The 3,000 houses "were almost entirely timber buildings, painted white, and this white much defaced by mud." There was one exception, he recalled, "in a red brick, two story residence in the north division." (Smith, *Cities of our Past & Present*, p. 53.)

10 In 1844 Joseph Goodrich built the Milton House inexpensively of "grout" consisting of slaked lime, gravel, sand, broken stone, and water, as well as lumber for the scantling and upper parts of the walls. Situated on the Janesville Road, the main road going north into the interior of Wisconsin, the Milton House was a busy stop in 1854 with as many as twenty-five stages arriving daily. Although it was called a tavern, Joseph Goodrich allowed no alcoholic drinks inside.

At the time Ellen and Willard arrived, the hexagon-shaped building was only two stories high with a long two-story wing attached. The parlor and kitchen area were on the first floor of the hexagon, the living quarters and guest rooms upstairs via a circular staircase in the center of the inn. Unbeknownst to its guests, the Milton House was part of the Underground Railroad. Connecting the cellar to a one-room log cabin behind the inn was a tunnel in which run-away slaves hid by day sleeping in the cabin at night on their way to Canada.

Believed to be the earliest grout structure in the United States, the Milton House remained in the Goodrich family until 1949 when it was given to the Milton Historical Society. After restoration, the building was opened to the public as a museum on May 1, 1954.

11 First-hand account of the first train that arrived in Madison on May 24, 1854, originally printed in the *Wisconsin State Journal*, May 24, 1854. (Mollenhoff, *Madison: A History of the Formative Years*, p. 51.)

12 L.M. Fuller and his family came from Vermont and settled in Sun Prairie, Wisconsin, in 1844. While Ellen and Willard were in Burke, Mr. Fuller was justice of the peace. Ellen and Willard's second cousin George Spaulding had built the Fuller house.

13 All mail and packages from her parents had been sent to George Spaulding at Token Creek. George's brother Nathan was the postmaster of Windsor, Wisconsin, for twenty-five years.

14 Abner's surname and relationship to the Spauldings is unknown at this time.

15 Esther Pitcher Bagley was the older sister of Thomas C. Bagley (Ellen's brother-in-law). At the time of the letter, Esther was thirty-one years old and staying with Thomas and Leonora Bagley at the brick house in Ludlow, Vermont. She had at least one child — Edgar, age three. Although records have not been found, from what Ellen wrote, Lewis Cline of St. Albans Bay, Vermont, had

asked Esther to marry him the following spring. There is a mystery as to this marriage of Esther's, however. On the quilt she is listed as "Mrs E Cline" living in St. Albans Bay, Vermont. Her son carries the surname "Cline." Possibly, Lewis Cline was a brother or relative of Esther's first husband (quilt block #34).

16 Many people from Ludlow, Vermont, settled in and around Janesville, Wisconsin.

17 Willard's family (his father, Joseph Reed, stepmother, Maria, brother Charles, half brothers Lucian and George, and half sisters Katia and Maria Leonora) all lived in Chelmsford, Massachusetts.

18 Because of the high infant mortality rate, babies were often considered temporary visitors. Depending on the practices of the individual family, many babies were not given names for months after birth.

19 The Cady brick house and land.

20 Leonora and Thomas's oldest child. He was five years old.

21 Dr. John-Quincy Adams married Sarah Lorinda Spaulding on August 15, 1853. The parents of Sarah Lorinda were Dolly Ives and Aaron Wheeler Spaulding, Stedman Spaulding's first cousin (quilt block #43).

22 Mr. Pettegrew was originally from Ludlow, Vermont.

23 One of the earliest settlers in Burke, he and his family lived on the same section of land as Willard and Ellen.

24 Mary Bagley was Leonora's sister-in-law (quilt block #41).

25 Maria L. Reed was half sister to J. Willard Reed (quilt block #6).

26 J. Willard Reed to Stedman Spaulding, from Burke, Wisconsin to Ludlow, Vermont, October 29, 1854.

27 Ellen E. Reed to Stedman and Arterista Spaulding, from Burke, Wisconsin to Ludlow, Vermont, October 27, 1854.

28 Delorma C. Bagley was Thomas Bagley's brother (quilt block #3).

29 Alden Patch, husband of Stedman's sister Sally (quilt blocks #27 and 28).

30 George Spaulding's daughter Lucy-Ann and her husband, George-Winston Harris. Only one year older than Ellen, Lucy-Ann was Ellen's third cousin.

31 Ellen E. Reed to Stedman and Arterista Spaulding, from Burke, Wisconsin to Ludlow, Vermont, November 19, 1854.

32 J. Willard Reed to Stedman and Arterista Spaulding, from Burke, Wisconsin to Ludlow, Vermont, January 7, 1855.

33 Ellen E. Reed to Stedman and Arterista Spaulding, from Burke, Wisconsin to Ludlow, Vermont, April 1, 1855.

34 Thomas and Leonora moved from Ludlow, Vermont, to Reading, Vermont, prior to March 11, 1855. Previously they had owned land and lived in Reading until April, 1853, when they sold their property and moved to Ludlow. While in Ludlow, Thomas, Leonora, and their children lived with Stedman and Arterista (quilt blocks #20 and 35).

35 J. Willard Reed to Stedman and Arterista Spaulding, from Burke, Wisconsin to Ludlow, Vermont, April 1, 1854.

36 Actually, Willard made a mistake and dated this letter "1854." Ellen's next letter of April 9 is correctly dated "1855."

37 Stoughton and Ivory Haven were Ellen's cousins (quilt blocks #25 and 26). They were sons of Ryland C. Haven, Arterista's brother (quilt block #19).

38 Mr. Howard was boarding with Ellen and Willard.

39 Polly Ross Riggs. Her daughter Mary L. Riggs is on Ellen's friendship quilt (quilt block #f).

40 Ellen E. Reed to Stedman and Arterista Spaulding, from Burke, Wisconsin to Ludlow, Vermont, June 8, 1855.

41 Stedman's father, Asa Spaulding. Asa's wife, Rhoda White, died in 1848 (quilt block #37).

42 Francis Wyman was married to Lois Spaulding, Stedman's sister.

43 James and Lydia Haven, parents of Arterista Spaulding (quilt blocks #18 and 15).
     Lydia Coleman Haven was the daughter of Solomon and Hepzebah Coleman, born in Ashburnham, Massachusetts, on January 25, 1786. She died August 25, 1858, six weeks after Ellen's death.

44 The men in the area would join together and go from farm to farm threshing until each of their farms were finished. The wife was very busy preparing enough food for all of the men while they were there.

45 Madison to Portage is about thirty-seven miles.

46 George Patch, Ellen and Willard's first cousin in Ludlow (quilt block #12).

47 George Spaulding's wife's maiden name was Mary Lawrence. Adelle's mother's married name is unknown at this time. Her maiden name was Lawrence.

48 J. Willard Reed to Stedman and Arterista Spaulding, from Burke, Wisconsin to Ludlow, Vermont, March 17, 1856.

49 J. Willard Reed to Stedman and Arterista Spaulding, from Burke, Wisconsin to Ludlow, Vermont, March 17, 1856.

50 The itinerant dentist came on horseback to Ellen and Willard's. It was a slow process drilling six teeth using a rusty hand tool and then filling them with lead or tin, but far worse, he pulled three more of Ellen's teeth without being able to deaden the pain.

51 Throughout her letters, Ellen used the words "comfortable" and "quilt" differentiating between the two. A comfortable was a quilt with a thicker batting, most likely of wool in the West, made for warmth and everyday use.

In 1843, Miss Leslie described comfortables in *The House Book* as "soft thick quilts, used as substitutes for blankets, and laid *under* the bed-spread. One of them is equal in warmth to three heavy blankets; and they are excellent in cold winters for persons who like to sleep extremely warm. In chambers with fire, or in a room that has had a fire all day, a comfortable will generally be found too warm a covering, except in severe weather. It is best to use them in cold apartments only. If the house should be crowded with guests, so as to cause a scarcity of beds, a thick comfortable may be found a convenient substitute for a mattress....

"A comfortable for a large or double bed ought to be three yards long and three yards wide. You may make it of glazed coloured muslin, (in which it cannot be washed,) or of furniture chintz, or cheap calico. It is best to have both the lining and the outside of the same material. Having run the breadths together, place it in a quilting frame, and lay on the cotton bats thickly and evenly, each one a very little over the edge of the other. A comfortable of the above size will require three pounds of carded cotton bats. It should be quilted in very large diamonds, laid out with chalk and a long ruler, or with a cord line dipped in raw starch, wetted to a thin paste with cold water. In quilting a comfortable, you need not attempt to take close, short stitches.

"In laying the cotton between the lining and the outside, leave *unstuffed* about half a yard on each side and at the bottom; but continue the stuffing quite up to the top or head of the comfortable. Let the thin part, however, be quilted the same as the rest. By thus leaving a thin border round the sides and bottom, you prevent the inconvenience so often objected to comfortables, their tendency to slip off the bed; as the thin part can be easily tucked in, so as to secure it perfectly from all danger of sliding out of place." (Miss Leslie, *The House Book*, pp. 313-314.)

52 Ellen and Willard's cousin George Alden Patch (quilt block #12).

53 On October 2, 1856, at 1 P.M. before S.C. Lyon, Justice of the Peace, and two witnesses, Willard got a mortgage on the land from the owner, Myron F. Lyon.

54 The nearest post office or postmaster was sixteen miles away at Mauston until July 16, 1857, when a post office was established at Fowler's Prairie in the Reuben Fowler home.

55 Leonora gave birth to her fourth child on December 19, 1856. He was named Frederick Herbert Bagley.

56 Lucy Eaton Haven, second wife of Ryland C. Haven (quilt block #c).

57 Charles and his wife, Emily, in Chelmsford, Massachusetts.

58 Commonly found in early New England homes, a buttery was next to the kitchen. It held many wide shelves on which flat crocks of milk were sat waiting for the cream to rise.

59 Wistar's Balsam of Wild Cherry, a compound of wild cherry bark and extract of tar, was a well-known, widely advertised "patent medicine" of the period. It was sold in an octagonal, aquamarine bottle by John E. Park of Cincinnati, Ohio, but because of its popularity, many imitations were sold as early as the 1840's. In 1851, Wistar's Balsam of Wild Cherry was advertised in newspapers by Park "for the instant relief and Permanent Cure of Asthma, Consumption, Coughs, Colds, Hoarseness, Influenza, Bronchitis, Bleeding of the Lungs, Difficult Breathing, Liver Affections, Pain and Weakness of the Breast or Side, Disorders of the Lungs and Chest." Professed to be "one of the oldest and most reliable remedies in the world," Wistar's was highly recommended by many doctors and ministers. (McKearin, *American Bottles & Flasks and Their Ancestry*, p. 299.)

Wistar's was available in Madison, Wisconsin, as early as 1855. J. Wright ran an add in the Madison newspaper, the *Daily Argus and Democrat,* on March 6, 1855, stating, "I AM THE only Authorized Agent in Madison, for the following valuable Medicines, and reliance cannot be placed on any purchased elsewhere. Be careful and obtain the genuine, as life might depend upon it." A list of medicines followed, including Wistar's Balsam of Wild Cherry.

60 Lucy-Ann Spaulding Harris, George Spaulding's oldest child, died of consumption two months later on March 15, 1858, at age twenty-four, leaving several young children motherless.

61 Whenever Willard went to Madison, he brought Ellen back fabric for a new dress. He had to go that far (nearly one hundred miles) for a good selection of dress goods.

62 Emily Emerson Reed, Charles Reed's wife, was twenty years old. She and Charles were living at 156 North Road, Chelmsford, Massachusetts, in the house that Emily's father built for them when they were married.

63 From Stedman Spaulding's pocket-size, leather-bound diary beginning August 21, 1854, and ending January 19, 1867.

64 Stedman Spaulding to Thomas and Leonora Bagley, from Glendale, Wisconsin to Reading, Vermont, July 15, 1858.

65 From Stedman Spaulding's diary, August 21, 1854 to January 19, 1867.

66 From his diary, Stedman "Paid Eld. Moor 1.00" for preaching Ellen's funeral.
   Reverend David Moore had come to Glendale, Wisconsin, in 1851. He was a circuit-rider minister from Oneida County, New York, where he had been ordained in 1840. There was no church building in the Glendale area, so Reverend Moore preached in log houses, the log school house, or any other available place.
   At the time of Ellen's death, he was living in a log house on a bluff two miles from Kendall, Wisconsin, and about four miles from Ellen and Willard's house.
   Descendants of David Moore are living in the Glendale area to this day.

67 Stedman's sister, wife of Alden Patch. She died two years later on September 28, 1860, and was the first to be buried in the plot with Ellen (quilt block #28).

68 The first post office in the area began July 16, 1857, in the home of Reuben Fowler and was called Fowler's Prairie Post Office. In 1861, Reuben Fowler became the first postmaster.

69 Lydia Coleman Haven died August 25, 1858 (see footnote #43).

70 Stedman Spaulding to Thomas and Leonora Bagley, from Glendale, Wisconsin to Reading, Vermont, August 18, 1858.

71 Horace Greeley, *New York Tribune*, December 25, 1858.

72 From Stedman Spaulding's diary, August 21, 1854 to January 19, 1867.

73 From Stedman Spaulding's diary, August 21, 1854 to January 19, 1867.

74 George Spaulding to Stedman Spaulding, from Burke, Wisconsin to Ludlow, Vermont, March 11, 1859. "Mrs. Spaulding" was Mary Lawrence Spaulding.

75 *The Mauston Star*, Mauston, Juneau County, Wisconsin.

76 Colonel Lyon was the postmaster in Glendale.

77 From Stedman Spaulding's diary, August 21, 1854 to January 19, 1867.

78 Willard W. Reed was born March 14, 1860.

79 Willard is talking about the Glendale property where he and Ellen lived.

80 Asa Spaulding had died February 9, 1860. Each of his grandchildren was to receive money from the estate. Stedman was in charge of the money.

81 J. Willard Reed to Stedman and Arterista Spaulding, from Plymouth, Wisconsin to Ludlow, Vermont, November 6, 1860.

82 J. Willard Reed to Stedman and Arterista Spaulding, from Plymouth, Wisconsin to Ludlow, Vermont, January 19, 1861.

83 "I suppose you have heard of Katies Death you know how to pitty us it was very hard to part with her but it was all for the best I suppose.... " Katie was Maria and Joseph Reed's seventh child to die. Maria E. Reed to Stedman and Arterista Spaulding (continuation of letter begun by Joseph Reed), March 21, 1860.

84 On October 14, 1861, George Eaton Reed, age twenty-three, enlisted in the 30th regiment Massachusetts Volunteer Infantry for three years. He was mustered in on November 30, 1861, at Camp Chase, in Lowell, Massachusetts.

85 Charles S. Reed to Stedman Spaulding, from Chelmsford, Massachusetts to Ludlow, Vermont, January 26, 1862.

86 Charles S. Reed to Stedman Spaulding, from Chelmsford, Massachusetts to Ludlow, Vermont, August 27, 1862.
     George Eaton Reed died of dysentery on August 2, 1862, at Baton Rouge, Louisiana.

87 Charles S. Reed enlisted in the Sixth Regiment Massachusetts Volunteer Infantry, Company K. He was mustered in on August 31, 1862. The regiment proceeded to Washington, then to Fort Monroe. They defended Suffolk, Virginia in the spring of 1863 and were in battle in Carrsville, Virginia, May 14-16, 1863.

88 Charles S. Reed to Stedman Spaulding, from Chelmsford, Massachusetts to

Ludlow, Vermont, August 27, 1862.

89   Joseph Reed was a very prominent man in Chelmsford, Massachusetts. Deeply religious and respected within the community, he was the innkeeper until 1856, as well as justice of the peace, representative, and selectman over the years.

From 1851 to 1864, Joseph, Maria, and their children lived at 1-3 North Road, the home where Willard lived prior to his going west. Joseph Reed had built the double cottage-style, clapboard house between 1840 and 1848. Joseph owned three other houses in Chelmsford during his lifetime: 65 Davis Road, 76 Westford Road, and 96 North Road, the home where he died. All but the tavern and store are standing today.

90   Willard W. born March 14, 1860; Katia M. born June 14, 1861; Almina J. born June 3, 1864.

91   J. Willard Reed enlisted as private in Co. E Forty-second Regiment of the Wisconsin Infantry Volunteers. He was mustered in at Madison, Wisconsin, two days later, on August 24, 1864.

92   J. Willard Reed to Stedman and Arterista Spaulding, from Camp Butler, Illinois to Ludlow, Vermont, January 10, 1965.

93   Mary Kenyon, "History of Glendale, Wisconsin," originally written for the *Kendall Keystone*. (Sent to author on typed pages by Tilmar Roalkvam, Elroy, Wisconsin.) Mrs. Kenyon also wrote, "All the men in the township were in the war with the exception of Col. Lyon, the postmaster, and Owen Richards.   Col. Lyon was the advisor and father of all the women and children of the community."

94   Ellen Spaulding Reed to her parents, from Glendale, Wisconsin to Ludlow, Vermont, July 18, 1857.

95   George Alden Patch was a very prominent person in the early development of Lathrop, Missouri. He was the first appointed depot agent, a job which he held until 1880. He served on the first Board of Trustees elected in 1869, and he was the first dealer in agricultural implements in the town.

He and Emma had two children, Warren W. and Mary E.

96   Stedman Spaulding to Arterista Spaulding, from Lathrop, Missouri to Ludlow, Vermont, November 4, 1878.

97   Willard has changed from talking about his parents in Chelmsford, Massachusetts, to talking about his daughter Katie and the rest of his family in Plymouth, Wisconsin. His half sister Katie, for whom he named his daughter, had died at age thirteen in 1860.

98 Stedman Spaulding to Arterista Spaulding, from Lathrop, Missouri to Ludlow, Vermont, October 27, 1878.

99 Stedman Spaulding to Arterista Spaulding, from Lathrop, Missouri to Ludlow, Vermont, November 4, 1878.

100 George A. Patch to Stedman Spaulding, from Lathrop, Missouri to Ludlow, Vermont, August 28, 1881.

101 George A. Patch to Stedman Spaulding, from Lathrop, Missouri to Ludlow, Vermont, May 8, 1882.

102 Katie M. Reed to Stedman Spaulding, from Lathrop, Missouri to Ludlow, Vermont, March 24, 1884.

103 Ellen E. Reed to Stedman and Arterista Spaulding, (continuation of letter begun by J. Willard Reed), from Burke, Wisconsin to Ludlow, Vermont, March 17-19, 1856.

104 Joseph and Maria E. Reed to Stedman and Arterista Spaulding, from Chelmsford, Massachusetts to Ludlow, Vermont, March 21, 1860 (quilt block #9).

105 Entry made on "National thanksgiving day," November 30, 1882. From Stedman Spaulding's diary of January 1, 1873 through July 31, 1884.

Bibliography

Genealogy and History

Adams, Henry K. *A Centennial History of St. Albans, Vermont.* St. Albans: Wallace Printing Company, 1889.

Aldrich, Lewis Cass, and Frank R. Holmes, eds. *History of Windsor County, Vermont.* Syracuse, N.Y.: D. Mason & Co., 1891.

Allen, Wilkes. *The History of Chelmsford.* Somersworth, N. H.: New Hampshire Printers, Inc., 1974.

American College of Genealogy. *History of the Wheeler Family in America.* Boston: American College of Genealogy, 1914.

Ames, Azel, M.D. *The Mayflower and Her Log, July 15, 1620-May 6, 1621.* New York: Houghton, Mifflin and Company, 1901.

Ancestral Chronological Record of the William White Family. Concord, N. H.: Republican Press Association, 1895.

Arber, Edward. *The Story of The Pilgrim Fathers, 1606-1623 A.D.; as told by Themselves, their Friends, and their Enemies.* New York: Houghton, Mifflin & Co., 1897.

Austin, H. Russell. *The Wisconsin Story.* Milwaukee: The Milwaukee Journal, 1949.

Bagley, Ernest Griffen, ed. *The Bagley Family, 1066-1958.* Raleigh, N. C.: 1958.

Bagley, Norton Russell. *Notes on Bagley Lines,* Vol. III. 1973.

The Bicentennial History of Milton. Milton, Wis.: The Milton Bicentennial Committee, 1977.

Biographical History of La Crosse, Monroe and Juneau Counties, Wisconsin. Chicago: The Lewis Publishing Company, 1892.

Case, Theodore Spencer. *History of Kansas City.* Syracuse, N.Y.: D. Mason & Co., 1888.

Chelmsford: A Historical Tour. American Bicentennial Edition, Chelmsford, Mass.: Chelmsford Historical Commission, 1975.

Child, Hamilton, ed. *Gazetteer and Business Directory of Windsor County, Vt. for 1883-84.* Syracuse: Hamilton Child, January, 1884.

Churchill, Mrs. Gordon, ed. *Cemeteries of Cavendish, Vermont.* Springfield, Vt.: Hurd's Offset Printing, 1977.

Cole, Arthur Charles. *The Irrepressible Conflict 1850-1860.* New York: The MacMillan Company, 1934.

Current, Richard N. *The History of Wisconsin: The Civil War Era, 1848-1873.* Madison: State Historical Society of Wisconsin, 1976.

Current, Richard N. *Wisconsin: A Bicentennial History.* New York: W.W. Norton & Company, 1977.

Drake, Samuel Adams. *History of Middlesex County, Mass.,* Vol. I. Boston: Estes and Lauriat, 1880.

Draper, Lyman C., ed. *Madison: The Capital of Wisconsin: Its Growth, Progress, Condition, Wants and Capabilities.* Madison: Calkins & Proudfit, 1857.

Dunbar, Seymour. *History of Travel in America.* New York: Tudar Publishing Company, 1937.

Earle, Alice Morse. *Home Life in Colonial Days.* New York: The MacMillan Company, 1966.

Ehrenreich, Barbara, and Deirdre English. *For Her Own Good.* Garden City, N.Y.: Anchor Press/ Doubleday, 1979.

Elroy. Bicentennial Committee of Elroy, Wisconsin, 1979.

Halacy, Dan. *Census 190 Years of Counting America.* New York: Elsevier/ Nelson Books, 1980.

Harris, Joseph N. *History of Ludlow,Vermont.* Charlestown, N.H.: Ina Harris Harding and Archie Frank Harding, 1949.

History of Ashburnham, Massachusetts. Ashburnham, 1887.

History of Dane County, Wisconsin. Chicago: Western Historical Company, 1880.

"History of Juneau County." Unpublished manuscript in the collection of Mauston Library, Mauston, Wis., March, 1927.

History of the Town of Westford, 1659-1883. Lowell, Mass.: Morning Mail Company, 1883.

Hollister, Hiel. *Pawlet for One Hundred Years.* Albany, N.Y.: Munsell, 1867.

Hunt, John Warren. *Wisconsin Gazetteer.* Madison: Beriah Brown, 1853.

Kellogg, Lucy Mary, ed. *Mayflower Families Through Five Generations,* Vol. I. General Society of Mayflower Descendants, 1975.

Kraus, Michael. *The United States to 1865.* Ann Arbor: The University of Michigan Press, 1959.

Land Atlas & Plat Book, Monroe County, Wisconsin. Rockford, Ill.: Rockford Map Publishers, Inc., 1980.

Lathrop, Missouri: A history assembled by the people of Lathrop. Lathrop, Mo., 1967.

Love, Wm. DeLoss. *Wisconsin in the War of the Rebellion; A History of All Regiments and Batteries.* Chicago: Church and Goodman, 1866.

Madison, Dane County and Surrounding Towns. Madison, Wis.: Wm. J. Park & Co., 1877.

Mansfield, David Lufkin. *The History of the Town of Dummerston.* Ludlow, Vt.: Miss A.M. Hemenway, Publisher, 1884.

Massachusetts Soldiers, Sailors, and Marines in the Civil War, Vol. I. Norwood, Mass.: Norwood Press, 1931.

Massachusetts Soldiers, Sailors, and Marines in the Civil War, Vol. III. Norwood, Mass.: Norwood Press, 1932.

Massachusetts Soldiers and Sailors of the Revolutionary War. Boston: Wright & Potter Printing Co., 1906.

Meadows, Mrs. Fanny L.S., and Miss Jennie M. Ames, eds. *Descendants of Reade or Reed.* Cleveland: Multigraphed by Jennie M. Ames, 1937.

McKearin, Helen, and Kenneth M.Wilson. *American Bottles and Flasks and Their Ancestry.* New York: Crown Publishers, Inc., 1978.

Mollenhoff, David V. *Madison: A History of the Formative Years.* Dubuque, Iowa: Kendall/Hunt Publishing Company, 1982.

Pollock, Paul W. *The Capital Cities of the United States.* Phoenix, Ariz., 1960.

Proctor, William Lawrence, and Mrs.W. L. Proctor. *A Genealogy of Descendants of Robert Proctor.* Ognensburg, N.Y.: Republican & Journal Print, 1898.

Randall, James G., and David Donald. *The Civil War and Reconstruction.* Boston: Little, Brown and Co., 1969.

Reed, Jacob Whittemore. *History of the Reed Family in Europe and America.* Boston: John Wilson and Son, 1861.

Report and Collections of the State Historical Society of Wisconsin, Vol. VII. Madison: E.B. Bolens, 1876.

Richards, Randolph A., ed. *History of Monroe County, Wisconsin: Past and Present.* Chicago: C. F. Cooper & Co., 1912.

Richardson, D.D., ed. "History of Glendale,Wisconsin," *Keystone,* Kendall, Wis.

Riegel, Robert E. *Young America, 1830-1840.* Norman, Okla.: University of Oklahoma Press, 1949.

Schafer, Joseph. *The Winnebago-Horicon Basin: A Type Study in Western History.* Madison: State Historical Society of Wisconsin, 1937.

Sherman, May Fowler. "Reminiscences of Elroy, Wisconsin." Written and read by her, age 81, at a ceremony on December 5, 1944.

Smith, Wilson. *Cities of our Past & Present.* New York: John Wiley & Sons, Inc., 1964.

Snyder, ed. *Historical Atlas of Wisconsin.* Milwaukee: Snyder, Van Vechten & Co., 1878.

Spalding, Samuel J. *Spalding Memorial: A Genealogical History of Edward Spalding, of Massachusetts Bay. And His Descendants.* Boston: Alfred Mudge & Son, 1872.

Statistics of Dane County, Wisconsin. Madison: Carpenter & Tenney, 1850.

Statistics of Dane County, Wisconsin: with a Sketch of the Settlement, Growth, and Prospects, of the Village of Madison. Madison: Carpenter & Tenney, 1852.

Stewart, Catherine. *New Homes in the West.* Readex Microprint Co., 1966.

Tuttle, Charles R. *An Illustrated History of The State of Wisconsin.* Boston: B. B. Russell, 1875.

Vexler, Robert I., and William F. Swindler. *Chronology and Documentary Handbook of the State of Wisconsin.* New York: Oceana Publications, Inc., 1978.

Vital Records of Chelmsford, Massachusetts to the End of the Year 1849. Salem, Mass.: The Essex Institute, 1914.

Vital Records of Hopkinton, Massachusetts to the Year 1850. Boston: New England Historic Genealogical Society, 1911.

Vital Records of Westford, Mass. to the End of the Year 1849. Salem, Mass.: The Essex Institute, 1915.

Wheeler, Albert Gallatin, Jr. *The Genealogical and Encyclopedic History of the Wheeler Family in America.* Boston: American College of Genealogy, 1914.

Wisconsin State Gazetteer and Business Directory, 1888-1889, Vol. VI. Chicago: R. L. Polk & Co., 1889.

Wisconsin Volunteers, War of the Rebellion, 1861-1865. Madison: Democrat Printing Company, 1914.

The World Almanac and Book of Facts 1981. New York: Newspaper Enter–prise Association, Inc., 1981.

Quilts, Costumes, and Other Textiles

Carlisle, Lilian Baker. *Hat Boxes and Bandboxes at Shelburne, Museum.* Museum Pamphlet Series, Number 4, Shelburne, Vt.: The Shelburne Museum, 1960.

Carlisle, Lilian Baker. *Pieced Work & Applique Quilts at Shelburne Museum.* Museum Pamphlet Series, Number 2, Shelburne, Vt.: The Shelburne Museum, 1957.

Cooper, Grace Rogers. *The Copp Family Textiles.* Washington: Smithsonian Institution Press, 1971.

"Essential Quilts, Exhibit at the State Historical Society of Wisconsin." Madison: State Historical Society of Wisconsin, 1980.

Fennelly, Catherine. *The Garb of Country New Englanders, 1790-1840: Costumes at Old Sturbridge Village.* Old Sturbridge Village, Sturbridge, Mass.: The Meriden Gravure Company, 1961.

Fennelly, Catherine. *Textiles in New England 1790-1840.* Old Sturbridge Village Booklet Series, Sturbridge, Mass.: The Meriden Gravure Company, 1961.

Finley, Ruth E. *The Lady of Godey's: Sarah Josepha Hale.* Philadelphia: J.B. Lippincott Company, 1931.

Frocks and Curls, the Clothing Industry and Women's Fashions from 1850 to 1900 in Hampshire County and Vicinity. Catalogue for an exhibit prepared by Carla Tscherny at Hampshire College, Amherst, Mass., August 25-29, 1978.

Godey's Lady's Book and Magazine. 1854-1886.

Hardingham, Martin. *The Fabric Catalog.* New York: Pocket Books, 1978.

Kunicov, Robert, ed. *Mr. Godey's Ladies (Being a Mosaic of Fashions & Fabrics).* Princeton: The Pyne Press, 1971.

Leslie, Miss Eliza. *The House Book: or, A Manual of Domestic Economy. For Town and Country.* Philadelphia: Carey & Hart, 1843.

Lord, Priscilla Sawyer, and Daniel J. Foley. *The Folk Arts and Crafts of New England.* Radnor, Pa.: Chilton Book Company, 1965.

Montgomery, Florence M. *Printed Textiles: English and American Cottons and Linens 1700-1850.* New York: The Viking Press, 1970.

Peto, Florence. *American Quilts and Coverlets.* New York: Chanticleer Press, 1949.

Pettit, Florence H. *America's Indigo Blues.* New York: Hastings House, 1974.

Pettit, Florence H. *America's Printed & Painted Fabrics.* New York: Hastings House, 1970.

Safford, Carleton L., and Robert Bishop. *America's Quilts and Coverlets.* New York: Weathervane Books, 1974.

Swan, Susan Burrows. *A Winterthur Guide to American Needlework.* New York: Crown Publishers, Inc., 1976.

Newspapers

Adrian Journal, Adrian, Mo., Thursday, March 2, 1933, and Thursday,
    January 31, 1946.

Daily Argus and Democrat, Madison, Wis., October 21, 1854, Vol. 4, No. 247;
    March 6, 1855, Vol. 4, No. 359.

"Life in Dane County Since 1847." *The Wisconsin State Journal*, Madison,
    August 13, 1925.

Lowell Weekly Journal, Lowell, Massachusetts, April 22, 1898.

The Mauston Star, Mauston, Juneau Co., Wis., November 20, 1857.

New York Tribune, December 25, 1858.

Primary Records Used

Census Population Schedules

United States Government. Federal Census 1870, 1880 and 1900.
    Clinton County, Missouri. Washington, D.C.

United States Government. Federal Census 1850. Hillsborough County,
    New Hampshire. Washington, D.C.

United States Government. Federal Census 1900. Douglas County,
    South Dakota. Washington, D.C.

United States Government. Federal Census 1850, 1860, 1870, 1880, and 1900.
    Windsor County, Vermont. Washington, D.C.

United States Government. Federal Census 1850 and 1860. Dane County,
    Wisconsin. Washington, D.C.

United States Government. Federal Census 1860 and 1870. Juneau County,
    Wisconsin.

United States Government. Federal Census 1860 and 1870. Monroe County,
    Wisconsin.

Wisconsin State Government. State Census 1855. Dane County, Wisconsin.
Madison, Wisconsin.

Cemetery Registers

Massachusetts	Forefathers' Cemetery, Chelmsford
Missouri	Austin Cemetery, Austin Crescent Hill Cemetery, Adrian Lathrop Cemetery, Lathrop
Vermont	Pleasant View Cemetery, Ludlow
Wisconsin	Fowler Cemetery, Elroy

Certificates of Death

Leonora A. Spaulding Bagley, October 11, 1912, Town
Clerk's Office, Weathersfield, Vermont.

Albert A. McWilliams, February 23, 1933, Bureau of Vital Statistics, Missouri
State Board of Health, Jefferson, Missouri.

Estella Reed, October 20, 1913, Bureau of Vital Statistics, Missouri State
Board of Health, Jefferson, Missouri.

Willard W. Reed, October 16, 1931, Bureau of Vital Statistics, Missouri State
Board of Health, Jefferson, Missouri.

Inventories

Estate of Leonora A. Spaulding Bagley, October 12, 1912, Vol. 61,
pp. 330-334, Probate Court of Vermont, District of Windsor, Vt.

Estate of Stedman Spaulding, April 23, 1885, Vol. 39, pp. 1-4, Probate
Court of Vermont, District of Windsor, Vt.

Marriage Records

Esther Bagley and Lewis Cline, Marriage records 1760-1870, Vital Records,
Montpelier, Vermont.

Land Transactions

"Abstract of Title"
>
> Concerning J. Willard Reed, December 12, 1853 to present, Section 24, Township 15 North, Range 1 East, Monroe County, Wisconsin.
>
> Concerning the Fowlers, Juneau County, Section 29, Vol. 131, p. 351, Vol. 21, p. 367.

Deeds. The Dane County Register of Deeds, Madison, Wisconsin,
> Section 28: Vol. 2, p. 26; Vol. 14, p. 194; Vol. 2, p. 25; Vol. 17, p. 337; Vol. 17, p. 338; Vol. 21, p. 7; Vol. 8, p. 561; Vol. 10, p. 191; Vol. 17, p. 487; Vol. 25, p. 352.

Land Records. (Thomas C. Bagley and Leonora Bagley) Vol. 18, p. 256, Reading, Vermont, April 6, 1853.

Mortgages. The Dane County Register of Deeds, Madison, Wisconsin, Vol. 2, p. 254.

Military and Pension Records

United States Government. National Archives and Records Service. Reed, Charles S., Co. K, 6th Massachusetts, (Union). Washington, D.C.

United States Government. National Archives and Records Service. Reed, George Eaton, Co. C, 30th Massachusetts, (Union). Washington, D.C.

United States Government. National Archives and Records Service. Reed, Joseph W., Co. E, 42 Wisconsin Infantry (Union). Washington, D.C.

United States Government. National Archives and Records Service. Reed, Joseph W., WC 728-943, Civil War. Washington, D.C.

Extensive Correspondence and Searches, including:

> Letters to all Bagleys in the Cavendish, Ludlow, and Rutland, Ver-mont areas for the descendants of Leonora A. Spaulding Bagley. Letters to all McWilliams in Kansas City, Missouri, for the descen-dants of Katie M. Reed McWilliams and information regarding her father, Joseph Willard Reed.

Index

Lyon, Myron, 77, 85-86, 93, 152-154

Madison, Wisconsin, 21, 22 and photograph; 25-26, 29-32, 34, 38, 40-41, 43, 45 46, 48-49, 51, 60, 64-66, 70, 74-75, 82, 101, 124, 165

Marriage, 20, 25-26, 35, 43, 55, 58, 68, 82, 147-149, 177-179

Mauston, Wisconsin, 85-86, 106, 112-113, 116, 123-124, 127, 148, 155, 162

McWilliams, Albert, photograph 17; 178, 186-187

McWilliams, Dr. Cline, photograph 17; 187

McWilliams, DeWitt, photograph 17; 187

McWilliams, Harland L., 16, 186

McWilliams, Katie M. Reed, photograph 16 and 17; 155, 159, 162, 166, 171, 172; letters 175-177 and 178; 179, 186; obituary 187; 188

McWilliams, Lucien, photograph 17; 187

Milkman, 173-174, 176

Mill, photograph 5; 21, 74, 82, 96, 99, 168, photograph 190

Milton House, 28, photograph 29

Milwaukee, 41, 101, 112-113, 127

Minnesota, 75, 77

Moore, Reverend David, 117

Motherhood, 25, 39, 46, 50, 67-68, 76, 109, 152, 162-163; naming of children 39

Neff, James, 93, 121, 153, 159

New York, 63

Ohio, 28, 45, 82, 178, 194, 196

Orphans, 67

Page, Mrs. L.M., 192, 195

Panic of 1857, 79, 91-128

Parker, Lorenda, 191, 194, 193, 196

Parker, Marcella, 193, 196

Parker, Nancy, 43

Patch, Alden, 6, 60, 168, 192, 195

Patch, Emma, photograph 168

Patch, George Alden, 83, 89, 98, 110, 168 and photograph; 169-174, 191, 194

Patch, Sally Spaulding, 121, 168, 192, 195

Pettegrew, Mr., 38, 39, 51, 123

Pioneer living, 34-35, 38, 41-42, 44, 54-55, 60

Plymouth, Wisconsin, 151-172

Proctor, Mrs. Betsey, 193, 196

Proctor, Harriet, 193, 195

Proctor, Mrs. M., 191, 194

About the Author

Linda Otto Lipsett is an internationally known quilt and women's historian. She is the author of *Remember Me* and *To Love & To Cherish*. Her years of extensive research and travels are evident in her books. Linda is also a professional violist who works in the motion picture, television, and recording industries in the Los Angeles area.

For additional titles write for our catalog.

Halstead & Meadows Publishing
P. O. Box 317211
Dayton, Ohio 45431